To my friend — Miss Allia — becoming someone who is becoming my favorite linguist. Because I saw the words companion, love, and light. Your friend — Sophia

Companion to Senya

by Senya Darklight
and Companions

edited by Marty Campbell

AAR
813.54
Darklight

copyright © 1989 Marty Campbell

ISBN 0-929749-01-4
Library of Congress Catalog Card Number: 88-92536

Mar Crafs, Frederiksted

AARW

Acknowledgements

I thank first the Park Wardens of Banff National Park, Alberta, Canada for your skilled and human sensitivity to me at this hard time and for your retrieval of Senya's two handwritten books. The books rested high up on the shelf of a cliff I could never have considered scaling myself and would not be included herein without the efforts of the Park Wardens.

Thank you and love to Senya's mother, Veronica B. O'Connor, and the entire family for your part in the environment from which Senya sprang and for your support of me in my life's readjusting and in my efforts toward this book.

For your support in all ways, thank you to my family in all its reaches, by blood and by marriage, re-marriage and adoption, including Lynnie and Mark who are with me always as pillars of spirit.

To Senya's friends and my friends and all the overlap.

Olu, Barbara, Cheza, and Afra. Cansee. Icah and Nesburn. Anet. Cenzo and Francesca. Who share the pace upon sacred ground. J. Mark Graffis and Winifred E. Eads for the steady keels of concerned friendship throughout. Carolyn Keys for her pre-trip fundraising efforts allowing balance to a dream and a friendship. The over one hundred personal and small business contributions over half-covering the publishing of this book!

Naima Wade Rodriguez of Quaking Grass Press,
Victoria Reck and Edmund Helminski of Threshold Press, and Peter Fietze and Lynn Holiday (then) of Caribbean Printing, for your invaluable conceptual advice and practical help in book design and printing.

John Jowers, Marie Daniel, and Sioux Faragher, of Virgin Islands Council on the Arts for your unceasing enthusiasm and helpful comments for this project.

The Curriculum Center of the Department of Education, under Ms. Karen Thurland, most especially Julio Espinosa and Sharon Jackson for your undying extension of resources and expertise toward my preparation of many drafts for this book and its fundraising appeals.

To Janell Agyeman for most helpful editing, Willie Myers for invaluable proofreading and fundraising consultation. Zena Cheza Dailey for proofreading and moral support, Audre Lorde for poetry publication consultation, and Ariane Krumholz for grant application consultation.

The list has no beginning and no end. All have given freely and with no mind to material benefit. This is the way of Senya.

Thank you.

This project received financial assistance from the National Endowment for the Arts through the Virgin Islands Council on the Arts

Contents

---

* As previously printed in <u>Rise in Love</u>.

** Page numbers in parentheses refer to the volume <u>SENYA</u> in his
    own handwriting.

List of Illustrations and Photographs

Cover: Senya, photograph by Clayton Jones.

p. xviii: Reproduction of the original "Fisher of Men"
text (typeset on p. 54).

p. 36: Barbara, Senya, and Cheza, left to right;
photograph by Sam Vaughan.

p. 40: The Stone Bird, St. Croix, north of Frederiksted;
photograph by Cenzo Colianni.

p. 73: Senya, photograph by James Weeks, Jr..

P. 94: Marty and Senya, photograph by Sam Vaughan.

p. 110: Marty and Senya,
photograph by Hedwig and Otto Larch.

p. 134: Reproduction of The Silent Flute,
by Deborah S. Howard, September 1987.
The original is 12" x 9" charcoal on paper, the first
of a series of drawings in response to learning of
Senya's death.

p. 154: Sky/lake photograph by Hedwig and Otto Larch.

Forward

As was his life wish, Senya was indeed a channel rather than a reservoir. Any gift he received flowed beautifully through him from one to another. His gift of spiritual attunement with the Most High glided so easily through him from the One to us all. All touched by his presence remain deeply affected.

Senya Darklight, named Anthony Michael Gerard O'Connor at birth, made a seemingly brief passage through this plane of life. Trinidadian, the fourth of ten children of Veronica and Thomas O'Connor, he was 20 when his family moved to Washington DC. After serving 2 years each in the Marines and the Navy, he worked several odd jobs and began performing poetry on the radio and otherwise. When he moved to St. Croix, he came clearly as a man of the spirit and a man of poetry. This is when I met him. He was 30. 1981.

Over his six years here on St. Croix, Senya performed oral poetry, accompanied with African instruments by himself and anyone willing, whenever and wherever asked. He made bamboo flutes and gave them to everyone interested. He kept a book during this time in which he wrote down pomes of particular import. [The spelling "pome" is a Marty-ism I am unable to shake. I include it here in this formal document against numerous appeals to the contrary. All I can do is say: I'm sorry.] Becoming very popular, he performed at schools at all levels, libraries, book shops, public functions, on radio, and on TV. He and I became fellow poets and close friends.

We at times fantasized about travelling across the U.S. giving poetry readings along the way. Though he thrived on the spirit, Senya was by intent not a man of physical means. When he won a roundtrip ticket to New York, we figured this was a sign to actualize our dream. He had taken First Place Overall in the Black History Month Poetry Contest, sponsored jointly by the Cultural Education Division of the Department of Education and Florence Williams Public Library here on St. Croix. This prize was for "School Shitstem burned out" (p. 25). (The original title as seen in the book SENYA is used here. For the purpose of contest entry, he had toned down this title to "The School System." Also, the rhythm rap chant chorus included both here and in SENYA was omitted in his contest entry.) Leaving in May of 1987, we indeed travelled across the States for three months, east to west, visiting family and friends and performing poetry at any slightest or most gallant drop of a hat.

A great friend, Olu, wanted very much to join us, with a video camera on his shoulder, but he was unable to. At his request Senya kept a written travelogue of the trip. Senya would often read from this at it's current stage of development at our performances along the way.

In chronological order, the complete text of Senya's poetry and travelogue is set in type for general readership in sections one and two of this book. This is the primary purpose of this book. He left us these words to pass on. Along with his bamboo flutes. He held little else. He desired little else. Spiritual attainment is the stuff of life to Senya.

The circumstances of Senya's passing are related in the third section, my completion to his travelogue.

Part four is a compilation of my writing over the years of our friendship as relates to Senya and to our trip together across the States. This is offered certainly not as a definitive study, but as the reflections of one individual with respect to another with the hopes of broadening the picture of Senya for those who did not know him.

Finally, part five is the collection of all the more or less formal writings that I know of at this time written in Senya's memory by various persons who knew him.

Editing

A book of his writing in his own handwriting has been published under the title <u>SENYA</u> and is available. Yet in typing his pomes for submission on several occasions, I have been amazed at the lyrical quality and precision that comes through so easily from sometimes apparent disorder. My desire here is to show this lyrical quality as clearly as possible. I want to also honor the key concern of Senya's that the greatest number of people, sophisticated and casual alike, be able to read the book easily.

Putting his writing to type has been both tough and joyful to me. As an oral poet, Senya did not always recite it the way he wrote it. He rarely read it. It was written inside of him. He in fact performed a given piece differently for each audience and occasion. He actually somehow spoke <u>to you</u>, magically, as if no one else were there.

In his own writing in the book <u>SENYA</u> it can be seen that he often made changes and sometimes left alternative words, with no clear choice. In these cases, I have set the word he used less often, in my experience, in parentheses beside the other. In one case ("The Rainbow Dancer", p. 37) I use a word he'd crossed out in place of the word he'd replaced it with because on the many occasions he recited it on our trip he used the crossed out word instead, and it *work*ed. Yet in the whole of both texts, changing the wording has not been necessary once! To me this attests to his tremendous writing power.

Senya was not a man bound by convention. In capitalization, punctuation, spelling, and line breaks, there is often inconsistency with no easily detectable pattern. I have tried to edit/correct each of these aspects only where it leads to confusion or misunderstanding. I have tried my best to do it as Senya would want it, following closely the guidelines we used in publishing together his first effort, Rise in Love; but, without his hand, making as few changes as possible. (In this process, I have prepared an almost complete manuscript of his poetry typeset exactly as he had it. Anyone wishing a copy in this form please write me.) The most dramatic changes occur in the shaping of the following pomes: "Ra Ru Mu Fa", "Journey Beyond All Forms", "Magenta Magic", "Most High F.M. Farther Mother", "The Rainbow Dancer", "What do you need?", and "Solo Sail", on pages 3, 4, 6, 20, 37, 38, and 44, respectively. For cross reference purposes in the poetry section, in the Table of Contents of this volume page numbers for each pome location in SENYA are in *parentheses* beside the respective page number for this volume.

The thirteen pomes from Rise in Love are reproduced just as they were, inserted in the chronological order in which they were written, and indicated by one asterisk in the Table of Contents.

In the travelogue, I have made line breaks and paragraph breaks according to the circumstances I know of his writing and according to the continuity in the episodes of our trip. Pages 113 and 124 in SENYA were entered by Senya after the fact and/or out of chronological sync. In attempt to keep chronological, poetic, and conceptual flows all intact, I have re-inserted them into what would be the bottoms of pages 114 and 128 of SENYA, respectively. This puts them on pages 78 and 81 in this volume. Similarly, in SENYA, the piece at the top of page 129 and a piece spanning 134-135 are both inserted at the top of page 133, putting them on page 82 in this volume.

In summary, my typesetting and edits have been with these intents: to clarify the special, even formal, lyrical quality of Senya's poetry and to facilitate general readability for as many readers as possible, hopefully not to the distraction or disrespect of any reader. There is danger in editing. But if *any*one is to edit Senya's writing, perhaps it is my obligation. I take this action only with heaviest responsibility in mind and deepest hopes that I have not clouded any precious aspect of this man.

Copyright

It was Senya's wish and intention that none of his work be copyrighted. To me, this stands on its own as a major statement of Senya's life. And so, though it has been a hard decision for me, I am honoring his wish on this. The material law was not a focus of Senya's. He would rather we exercise another law, the law of the heart, the law of spirit: that we feel completely free to copy his work in any portion for any positive purpose, and from the respect in our own heart to copy it correctly, without change. Perhaps now, also, to give credit by including his name, as source, on the copy, though Senya would claim the original source to be otherwise: "It's all the Most High."

Those of us involved with sharing Senya's work ask that credit be given to him and that any profits be shared in part with the Senya Fund. This fund to aid young Caribbean poets is being established by friends of Senya's through Bamboula Haven Foundation, Inc. (Box 5676 Sunny Isle USVI 00823-5676) on St. Croix.

One anecdote that still sparks my amazement perhaps relates well to the issues of copyright and publishing. After I had known Senya only a short while—long enough to know how I treasured his words—he confided in me the following episode and the attached rationale. "You know, not long ago I offered up a portion of my poems that I had written down—to the whole world. I gathered them together on their various papers, and I took apart a little book of them, so it could catch more easily, ... and I offered them up in a great fireburning." There was a pause here where I assure you I said nothing. I was stunned. Another friend of mine had done the same thing. I am still incapable of comprehending such an action. I am sure that even my stare did not move, when Senya continued, "The smoke was tremendous. It went straight up, through the trees, and mixed into the atmosphere. It is sure that ashes have settled in many many places all over the earth, and people have been touched by my poems who would never otherwise have had the chance." The words are mine—these are not direct quotes—but this is the gist of what he said. I am still amazed. But as amazed as I am, I feel it likely, that as you read through these pages you will recognize something very familiar, and perhaps not know from where.

And so it is that having full knowledge of Senya's method of publication I have the gall to publish two versions of his writing in print, thousands of copies! Of course I have also the experience of our publishing his booklet Rise in Love together. And that was a success. Senya passed them out like a stateside tree passing out its

xiv

leaves of gold in the fall—one to everyone who wished. And I sold enough to pay back the printer. Many many people still hold them as ever-refreshing treasures.

Why should there now be two versions of his complete works: SENYA in his own hand, and Companion to Senya typeset? As noted above, I have been fascinated with how the pomes fall so easily from what sometimes look like almost random placements of words into clear, near traditional, lyrical patterns and shapes. To me, the two read like two completely different books, each with a particular beauty of its own. It is like trying to release at least two dimensions of a very multidimensional man—a man who defies dimension, ... in his "journey beyond all forms" (p. 4). It is my hope and my belief—and my wish to have available to all who might—that many readers will share my joy and excitement at mingling and endulging in both forms.

There are still other forms. Senya made several cassette tapes for meditation and innerattainment, and several sound recordings were made of his readings. Further, there are a number of videos, both professional and amateur, in which Senya is featured. Efforts are being made by people versed in these media to produce copies and compilations for those who wish them. Anyone interested may contact me. I will forward requests to the right persons. There have also been live performances as widely dispersed as Vermont, Philadelphia, Buffalo, and St. Croix, of artists with their own interpretations of Senya's work. And there are rumors of a T-shirt. Keep your eyes open.

Word Usage

A few notes may be in order with respect to word usage in specific pomes. Right off the bat Senya hits us with "Ra Ru Mu Fa" (p. 3). That's the title. Then follow a whole string of words with meanings that probably require wide general knowledge, mainly spiritual, to understand. I will not pretend to tell you their dictionary, spiritual, or even distinctly-Senya meaning. I would rather encourage you to do the research and settle on your own understanding. But I will try to lead you in a few good directions: "Chi", "omm", and "Ra" have very special and deep spiritual significances perhaps both in the ancient African and the Far Eastern traditions. In the later pome "CHE OM RA" (p. 64), they refer also to his cat with that name. "Isis" is the name of the chief goddess in African spiritual traditions. "Nzinga" is the name of a great African Queen. "Kilima Njaro" is Senya's way of spelling the name of the highest mountain in Africa, denoting that it is, with the people there, two distinct words, each with its own special meaning.

"Zebu" is the name of an African breed of cattle, predominantly white, with high shoulders. This breed was introduced to St. Croix, and some broke through their fences and live wild in small herds throughout the hills where Senya resided. All have been serenaded more than once by Senya's flute. They made their way through the very thickest of bush, graciously providing paths of access to any location Senya wished to visit. That they were African, that they were wild, that they were companions on the same land, made them special to Senya.

"Sirius" is a star of great significance to Senya. He focuses in on it in the pome, "Sirius," (p. 14).

"Maroon" is a term used widely throughout the black diaspora of the Caribbean Islands and South and Central America to refer to those blacks who successfully escaped from slavery and set up their own communities, usually in the most inaccessible terrain available. There was such a community here on St. Croix, and were also on most of the islands throughout the Caribbean, and also on mainlands. This is not so apparent in "history" books, but becomes quite apparent on visiting each area and speaking with what remaining segments of culture there are that care about such details. Senya cared deeply.

Referred to in "Redemption in I(Ay) I(Ay) U.C.A. M20" (p. 29), "U.C.A. M20" is the title of an organization of people with strong heartfelt African identity, centered in Frederiksted, with a headquarters affectionately known as "Stand Up." Spelled out, it is "United Caribbean Association" and has its anniversary of formation on May 20th. "Freedom City" is the affectionate name held by many for Frederiksted, the seat of the announcement of the freedom of slaves here in the then Danish West Indies, and in general a town with a longtime reputation for freedom of spirit. "Ay Ay" (pronounced "I-I") is the original name given St. Croix by the people, so called "Indians", living here before Christopher Columbus and the Western world arrived. "I and I" is the Rastafarian term meaning "all of us," or I as representative of the whole body in faith.

"Stone Bird" (p. 41) refers specifically to a fixed stone sticking up by itself out of the water beside Senya's favorite sea swimming location north of Frederiksted. It is shaped just as he describes it, as if it is a bird taking off in flight. Of course, now that you know that definition, don't let it limit any possible meaning you might get from the pome!

"INografi(e)" (p. 59) stands there on the page by itself. I leave it there for the reader to go with. I offer this vein: I believe it roots on a play with the word "geography", only substituting the "I" as in "I and I" as discussed above or the "In" of "within" for the "geo". And perhaps the "I" again at the end. Senya loved maps and books about other parts of the world. He felt they were a means of travel. He knew as much about places he'd "never been" as about the very place he lived. Perhaps here in this pome-word he is suggesting we each chart the maps of the worlds within our selves. I believe it merits a whole page. I'm not sure if he ever intended otherwise.

In his travelogue, Senya refers to the "horizon." This could refer to many things—one thing being the car we were loaned for the whole of the trip by my father. It was the model "Horizon."

"Kilima Njaro" appears in one other very special place. This is in the long story-pome "Journey to Kilima Njaro (Cloud Mountain)" (p. 34). This was a most dear piece to Senya. He offered it up very carefully only to audiences he hoped were "ready for it" and very thoroughly/completely when he did. Explanations and anecdotes would come out along the way. I never heard it the same way twice. So far as I know he never wrote it down in full. A small nuclear, or seed, portion appears in his own hand in SENYA (p. 41). I took it by dictation for inclusion in Rise in Love (centerfold, fully illustrated by his own artwork). It is in this latter full form that it appears here, to many of us his masterpiece.

Here, it is all bundled together, offered up in another—I hope just as gentle—form of smoke.

Marty Campbell
Box 2565 Frederiksted
USVI 00841-2565

Fisher of Men

boundless boat of light

one
Man in a
in sound

Pull in a net, of Mann

Birds of all types to be seen
on there Islands circle overhead.

boat
They take in the   Man

Women in children of all types
and Colours to be seen on there islands

All Way up over the rainbow,
to home of eternal Sunrise.
Sail Sail   on light in sound

Sail on fisher of Men

I. Poetry

Ra Ru Mu Fa

Night fire still burns, smoke is in the air.

At dawn the light bird comes

dancing on rainbow wings.

Echos of air fire water earth, Dolphy, Sirius, Maroon,

Chi omm Ra, Ra omm chi, Ra I(eye)sis, Nzinga,

Kilima Njaro, Zebu, golden hawk,

All on peacefull mountain, Harmony is Home.

Light bird has come.

Blow, Wind, make a joyfull Sound.

Journey Beyond All Forms

Hear the Universal heart beat,

Feel the flow of life's breath eternal,

Alive but unborn, unformed, unseen,

Yet seeing all, through the eye Most High,

In the center of life's boundless circle,

All share breath with the great spirit.

Breathe deeply as one journey

Beyond all forms.

Life Dance

All forms do the dance of life,

Be they large or small,

All move in harmony

To the Most High call,

Still there are some dancers

No one sees at all.

Magenta Magic

I saw Magenta in the sun rise one morning,

And for me I knew a new day was dawning,

Free from the worlds of changing illusions,

By divine (god)goodness I've

transcended pain and confusion.

I saw false self die and true self born.

Now agony is gone, I am no longer twisted

and torn.

Somehow I knew this birth would come

because at dawn I heard a beat from

the Universal drum.

Magenta such a brilliant ray gave onto

I an eternal day. This is real magic I say.

Mountain Most High

' Ol Doinyo he N,gai '

in Tanganyika is Mountain of
the god, crowned with clouds and
Rainbows of sunlight,

Magestic mountain of volcanic
ash, adorned with many ravines
where water runs when dark
clouds bring blessings of ancestral
Rains giving an earthly body
a heavenly wash,

Ol Doinyo he N,gai
Mountain of the Most High

Love Drought

here we are waiting on a blessing

of spirituall rain,

to wash away all physical mental and

emotional pain,

again an again we wait in vain

but the Most High rain won't

come until we Live the will

of (good) Jah, and truly love one

in all, open your heart and feel

the rain fall, let love flow

put a end to this drought,

Tribute to Baobab Tree

CHORUS

CHORUS:

Bara Bara, Bara Bara,
Bara Bara, Baobab
Baobab Baobab Baobab
Baobab Bara

O! Great Baobab, root of our ancestral tree,
Where griots go to see,
You grow such powerful fruit for we.
Strong with song, now we free.
Show us where we must be.

CHORUS

Oh Great Baobab, your branches like roots reaching for the sky,
Baobab, you make my spirit high,
When I see you growing in Ay Ay,
Right side up lookin upside down
Baobab, you help me sing life song

CHORUS

Oh Great Baobab, when we were searchin for wisdom,
We found it in the water you hold in your trunk.
Now we drink this water of life we never thirst no more.
In you we have what we were searching for.

CHORUS

Earthly Delights

A state of bliss.
Tis truly good fortune
To be blessed like this.
Everything needed to be in tune
With life's eternal time,
Infinite light manifested in form,
Vibrations flowing from the womb
    of the unborn.
Be sure to appreciate and
Participate in the vision of now,
Because when we transcend
    this plane,
Unless we be born as a child
    again,
We can no longer enjoy these
Earthly delights.
Heavenly delights, here we come.

Timeless People

There is a land called timeless
it's on the plain of the inner world
here past present and future is one
everything happens right on time,
The timeless people are never late
The time less people don't have to wait
they are expressions of yesterday
today and tomorrow, in the moment
of the eternal now,
all the people on this earthly plane
use to live in the timelessland
but we developed turbulent minds
and, due to unharmonious thought
vibrations, were expelled

as you all know everything
moves in cycles, So we are now
at a point where we can
rejoin the people of timeless land
to do so we must know ourselves
so we can harmonize our little
minds with the great all inclusive
total divine mind of the
Cosmic One, within whom we
all live move and have our
being

in time we will all be timeless
in tune with the Timeless One

Creatures of Ay Ay
Morning Meditation

The sun is risin over the hilltops as a group
of 9 white birds fly east over the valley on
their way to have breakfast with the cows.
Pearl-eyed thrushies chase each other
playfully through the trees at breakneck
speed.
Humminbirds visit nearby flowers and zoom on.
Bananaquits, grass quits, chincherees, zenida
dove, ground dove, bridal quail doves; blue,
redneck, and white crown pigeons, all make
joyful sounds.
The morning air is pierced by 3 screamin
cries as a pair or red tail hawks glide
overhead.
I hear the laughter of the coo coo bird,
followed by a tribe of black birds wailin
like jungle sirens.
A community of ants enlarge their
subterranean dwelling and pile up the fine
textured gold colored earth around their
doorway.
Elaborate spiderwebs covered with dew reflect
the morning sunlight.
All the colors of the rainbow can be seen.
Look over there, a family of mongoose playin
in the tall Guinea grass.
There are lizards everywhere, making sounds
we cannot hear.
I see a large adult lizard facing the sun,
busily doing what appears to be yoga
exercises, as his throat extends 2 inches
from the body displayin bright orange.
As I walk along the footpath, I encounter a
hermit crab becoming aware of my presence.
He or she withdraws into the shell, leaving
the tips of 3 feet and a long purple and
orange clipper exposed.
As I meditate on the crab, I come out of my
shell. Just another creature on Ay Ay.

12

Rise in Love

Why do we fall in love
When we can rise in love?
We don't need a falling love,
We need a rise in love.
A love that will take us higher
So we achieve what we aspire.

Many fall in. Many fall out.
Come let us rise without a doubt.
A Devine love will raise our
    vibrations,
Keep us in harmony with the
    Most High meditation.
Love is a high, not a low.
So don't fall in, that's not the way to go.
Love is the main ingredient
    in this life recipe.
The devine dish won't be right
    without your L.O.V.E.

Sirius

Brightest Star by Far. Shining light
lead us where you are.
From the dog days of summer to the
middle of winter I see your beams of
light each and every night.

I heard you have a smaller companion
that orbits around you, revolving nine times
to your one.

In mythology you are said to be the
dog that follows the hunter Orion.
And the Dogon people of Mali say
that it's from you they came as beams
of life taking human form upon the
earth.

Indeed you are a lodge of light
big sun, way upon high, truly the
brightess diamond in the sky

Web of Cosmic Consciousness

like a falling leaf stopped by a
        Suspended Spider Web,

like Wise a soul falling
        into the Material Worlds of illusions
        Can be stopped by the divine Web
        of Cosmic Consciousness,

for all is the being of the Most High.

we are beams of light life n love Radiating
from the one central sun that is
the all seeing eye in the Web of
Cosmic Consciousness.

all is the Most High

Wish to Know

As we live this life and wish to
know we have to see the signs
that show.

There are signs in the water
signs in the wind
signs in the earth
signs in the fire

All calculated to take us
Higher.

It's all the Most High

When someone is born or someone dies
We have to remember it's all the Most High.
For birth and death are but illusions of life eternal.

Regardless of how we view
people places or things as good or bad
and the situations that we allow
to make us happy or sad,
We have to remember it's all the Most High.

Definitions of good or bad are generally
based on emotional judgements and not
in the light of the law of cause and
effect. Retribution.

So let us, as one, remember all is one
it's all the Most High   ◉

Freedom City Voices
Rising in harmonious sound
Melody of music
Take us where we belong,
Finding all that was lost
In a simple sound.
United in I ay I ay Voices of Victory
rise free

Sea Secrets

How many secrets can the sea hide
Beneath its waves and ever changing
   tides?
There must be millions of places
To hide lost treasure beyond measure,
Pieces of life's past puzzle presently
   revealed,
In the fragments of a trillion
   yesterdays,
To be found in the sand.

So when walking along the beaches
   of your mind,
Stop, look, listen, sometime,
So you can come to know
The secrets of the sea.

Most High F. M. Farther Mother

All praises due to the Masculine
Feminine aspects of our Creator
Most High.

Praises O Divine Farther Mother.

Thanks for the blessings of my earthly farther n
mother and the three sons and seven daughters
that came out of their union.

I am thankfull for my brothers n sisters all over the earth,
as numerous as the sands of the sea.
They bring much joy into this heart.

And to see their shining presence before me,
all in the Image of my divine Farther and Mother
is truly a great blessing. Give thanks.

May Day
Relation Ship Wrecks

All over the earth relation ships
are struggling to stay afloat on
a stormy sea of emotions.

Waves of unfulfilled expectations
hide the sharp reefs of
disappointment.

On a clear day, if you journey along
the coastline of emotionland, many
relation ship wrecks can be seen.

Sometimes when the waters of my
mind is calm, I hear the voices
of drowning souls sending
S.O.S. to the Most High.

I wonder why they wait so late
to call for devine guidance.

O Most High though we have been
so unloving to each other, be it
thy will to guide us still.

See Sun. See I

I see sun, Sun see I
I am Sun, Sun is I
See I, See Sun, See On

feeling fools

emotional feelings fool us.
feeling up feeling down,
sometimes a smile sometimes a frown,
feeling glad feeling mad,
feeling feelings we wish we never had,
being enslaved to moods that make us happy or sad,

feeling young feeling old,
feeling like silver feeling like gold,
feeling love feeling hate.
if you want to get to heaven
don't let feelings make you late.

what about feeling, it's time to stop
feeling, and just be

Free up, Open your heart

Take a deep breath for a start, be at ease

in each moment, allow your self to relax.

Don't think of yesterday or tomorrow

just face the present facts.

Say open sez me, to the doors of your soul,

and resurrect your self

from the drugged sleep of material love.

Let us raise our energies from the

lower worlds of death, to the realms

of life above.

School Shitstem burned out

Rythm rap
chant chorus:

    a chi chi huh huh
    it's a mad mad world
    don't let it get
    your little boy or girl.

a chi chi
huh! huh!
pap! pap!
pa! pa!
pap! pap!
a chi chi
huh huh
it's a mad mad world
don't let it get
your little boy or girl

Passin by Middle School on Central High Road
See my sisters and brothers bein conditioned to carry
       this world's heavy load
Rappin, Scrappin, Crappin at recess time
Tryin to find a reason in the rhyme
Spinnin around with their minds in a maze
Practicin the latest moves of the break dance craze
Like wind up toys our girls and boys
Are dancin on a tight rope with no net below
Way way up, under the big top
Just characters in the circus of life
They have to deal with trouble they have to deal with
       strife
When they finish school with no home rule
Still standing in line, they can't get no job
They got to come out in the street and face an angry mob
So they hustle and they bustle, movin too and fro
Beginnin to realize they ain't got nowhere to go
Just look at this society's sad side show
Projects and prisons are bein put up
No one knows when this madness gonna stop
I think on it a little, and I shake my head
I'm just movin on this earth with the livin and the dead.

BACKGROUND
CHANTING:

Ah! huh huh huh huh
I Aye! ya yay Oh! Oh! Oh!
Island in the sun
Got you on the run
Ay Ay Ay
Ay Ay Ay

Island on the Run

Ah! Here you are on an island in the sun,
But the struggle to survive can keep you on the run.
You would like to take the time to help some one,
But when your work is over the day is done.
It's supposed to be a paradise,
But the prices you must face can bring tears to your eyes.
Fighting the traffic to get home and fix some dinner,
You have a little herb so you feel like a winner.
None of your children greet you at the door,
To look at t.v. seems to be what they are living for.
Looking in the mirror as you change your clothes,
Brings your body ain't what it used to be.
Your mind down to earth to face your woes.
You may not be looking too healthy,
And you wonder how much the people can see.
If you have a boil on your bamcee about to bursty
And you go to a doctor, he may make matters worse,
Alone in bed, you can toss and turn all night,
Having a dream that shows you things just not right.
In the dream an island in the sun got you on the run.

Rainbow Hill

⊙ !   Great Central Sun Single
emanating eye of the Divine one,

Praises for the blessing of thy aura's
image hovering over rainbow hill.

As dawn breaks, last night's full moon
appears to be heading west, as the earth
Revolves eastward, the jewel eye at
the centre of this system, in the likeness
of the great Central Sun of cosmos, seems
to be on the rise once again.

Mourning doves, Mountain pigeons, and roosters
all salute the approaching rays of daylight,
enraptured in the echos of nature's
Musical Vibrations, I hear the voice
of divinity deep within, Saying

Arise, O! earthly son, do the will of
your heavenly farther, serve those who
serve him.

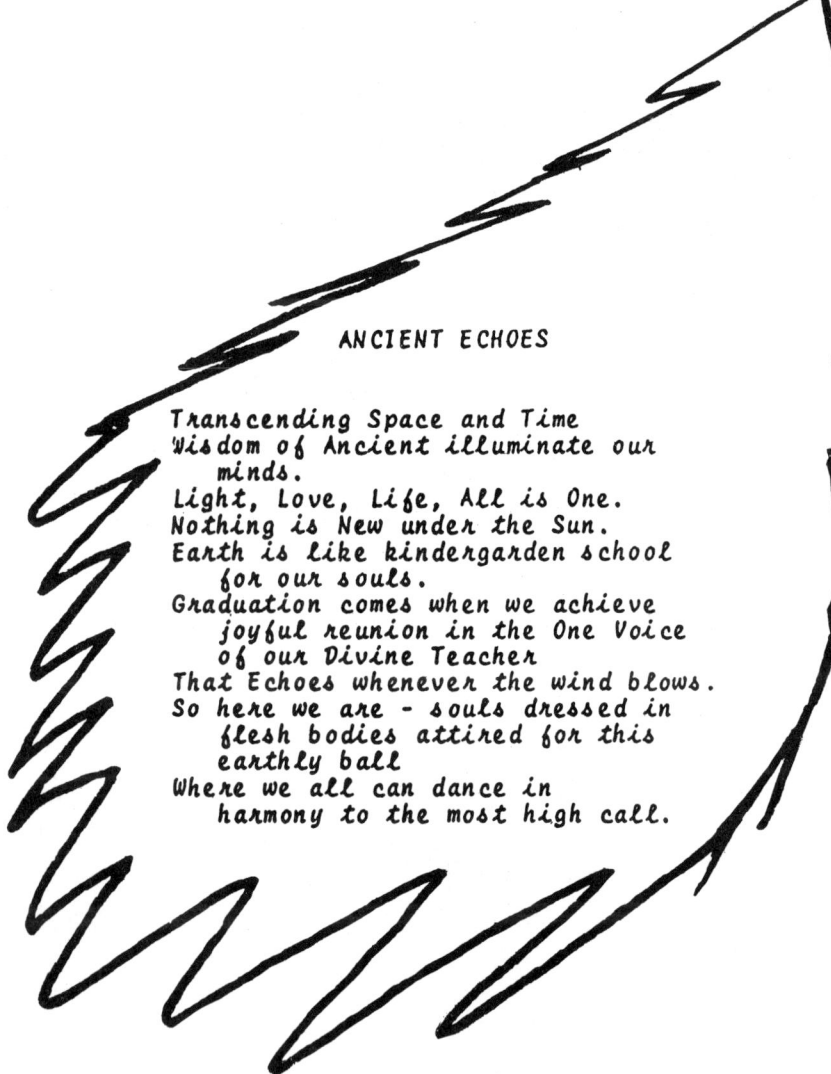

ANCIENT ECHOES

Transcending Space and Time
Wisdom of Ancient illuminate our
    minds.
Light, Love, Life, All is One.
Nothing is New under the Sun.
Earth is like kindergarden school
    for our souls.
Graduation comes when we achieve
    joyful reunion in the One Voice
    of our Divine Teacher
That Echoes whenever the wind blows.
So here we are - souls dressed in
    flesh bodies attired for this
    earthly ball
Where we all can dance in
    harmony to the most high call.

Redemption in ⌉Ay ⌉Ay U.C.A. M20

A bright shining light in freedom
city illuminating the road home free.
On this your 15th Anniversary, standing as firm
as can be. Let me tell you what you
mean to me.

You are like a Majestic Sistar
a queen of light
beaming your love through out
the Universe, becoming a mother
to us All while still in the dawn
of your days, and schooling our
children in Ancient African Ways.

U.C.A. you are the one who prepared
a place for I in I in Ay Ay.

Praise to the one who brought you
forward like a baby from a dream to
reality. U.C.A. you are the one who
keep on shining like the sun and
We are your children.

Stand up for Iver.

see it

A leaf fell from a book of
poetry. I observed it dancing
in the air to land at my feet.
It reminded me of a leaf I
had seen falling from a tree
last night, walking along
a road lined by giant
Mahogany trees,
                            I saw what
appeared to be a star falling
from the heavens, but when
I looked up and counted
them, none was missing.

I don't look in the mirror
when I want to see my
Image, I look in your
eye.

Within

There is light and color
See it
Within
There is sound
You hear it comin and goin
Yet it is always here
Flowing in an endless stream
The reality of life's dream.
On the mountain of peace
The dove of love is at rest.
Worlds within each other
Like bubbles
Within bubbles
Within
Love

Love Rain

The land has been hot and dry
for many moons,
on the wind I feel hear and
smell the approaching Rain of
Love.

Life is calling for the rain
birds fly to and fro making joyfull
sounds, all growing forms reach
in and out embracing rain
dancing in love.

Rain drinking up the earth and
bursting out of springs streams
and Rivers Rushing to kiss the sea
going up and comming down
all over again
                    Love Rain

OF All Nations Peoples and Religious

organizations There is not one among

them all that can show a bill of

Sale for any thing signed by God

and yet they still kill maim Frame and

blame one in other all in

the names of the Most High

Journey to Kilima-ñjaro

So many of my sisters and brothers
Scattered all over the earth
Are tired of cleaning houses they do not live in
Tired of washin cars they do not drive
Tired of guardin property they are not allowed to use.
Those who do not possess anything have nothing to lose.
They are the ones closest to freedom.
Total liberation is the next step to take.
The harvest of the earth is due.
And the forces of light are prepared to reap love and life.
In the distance I hear voices chanting,

> Africa we comin over
> Home we comin
> Mother we comin
> Ay yea yea wo A wo
> Ay yea wo A wo ay yah.

We comin from New York Shitty
Where people have no pity.
Comin from Chicago
Where they have plenty cars but they can't go.
Home we comin.
Comin from Califony
Where everything is all so phony.
Comin from the Caribbean
Where we've been carried beyond.
We comin from Ay Ay,
Yea we comin from Saint Cry.
Home we comin.
We leaving these worlds of trouble and strife
Where we almost lost our light
Going to a place of happiness and peace.
Come with us to the East
Where our elders dance and sing
Far away from death's sting
They see life's beauty beyond everything.

> Africa we comin over
> Home we comin
> Mother we comin
> Ay yea yea wo A wo
> Ay yea wo A wo ay yah.

Kibo Mawenzi Mawenzi Kibo
Two peaks of Kilima-njaro
We are journeying on a vibrational vehicle of musical sound
Going where we all come from
To the womb of the earth
By the Great Riff Valley
And the lakes from which the Nile flow.
We have arrived at the foothill of Kilima-njaro
Where we greet the people of Chaga Land.
And the elder of the village speaks to us saying,

"Sisters and Brothers, Sons and Daughters,
Welcome.
In the village of life there is a sacred place.
It is known as the Temple of Love.
Through these portals must pass all mortals
To gain entrance to the fountain of life everflowing
Through faith each and every one can overcome the wall of fear.
For it is only a picture subconsciously projected
On the screen of our minds.
By seeing all life through our Most High eye
We can avoid the traps of vanity
By not worshipin physical beauty.
For all images of material things appear only for a time.
Unlike the spirit of all beauty that is true reality
And can endure the changin forms of life and live forever.
The road of material gain can lead to spiritual loss
For all that we claim to possess truly possesses us.
It is our thoughts that imprison our minds.
And when this fog of forgetfulness fades away
Then we shall see the temple of love
And know the origin and destiny of all life.
For as it is in the eye of a hurricane there is a calm
So in the turmoil of the worlds
Peace can be found in the spirit of all beauty.
So respect your teachers, regardless of how they teach.
If you follow the path of love, eternal life you will reach."

Oh great wind, my faithful friend
Take this message wherever you sing
Beyond mountains standing tall
All shall listen when you call.
Unite these seas of separation with this message of unification.

The highest mountain in Africa
Is symbolic of the highest within you.
The snow-capped peak of Kilima-njaro
Represent the purity of heart all must attain.
So remember wherever you are
Kilima-njaro Kilima-njaro
The mountain of the clouds is within you.

Kilima-njaro-oh-o-oh-o-oh-o
Kilima-njaro-oh-o-oh-o-oh-o
Kilima-njaro-oh-o-oh-o-oh-o

Once in a blue Moon

Your laughter is bliss to me

Such a brilliant flower of infinite

beauty, to behold a flash of light in

sound in Full bloom,

like two full moons happening

in one month, once in a blue moon

The Rainbow Dancer

I/eye come from a place of inner space

in there among your Stars.

In the brightest star you see at night

you'll see you if you're lookin right.

The Jungles of the Mind

The bush of fear exists only
in the jungles of the mind. When we
enter deep therein and overcome
the savage beast of ego,

then we are free to journey
from the dismal regions of
Darkness, Disease and Death
to the paradise of
Life, Light, and Love.

Come let us go in to moments
of silent meditation and
rise above all outer trials
and tribulation

What do you need?

When you know your needs,

The needs of All will be known.

You see them reflected

In the clear Still Waters of your Soul.

twilight

As the earth dances to

Celestial Sound the sun

seeams to wink goodnight

Kissin other spaces with

light, there is music all

around, huming birds Kiss

papaya flowers in the

twilite a flute plays (in) for

the sunrise

Soul Music

We are all flutes through us

god makes eternal music

   Can you hear the sound.?

Turn down the boom box of

your mind and listen in to

   the music of your soul

Stone Bird

The wind and sea has

shaped a bird on the reef.

There it is starein at the

distant horizon. Look

quickly, it's about to fly away.

Remember the time

We followed the sunset into the night

driving along winding reddish

clay roads leading who knows

where, the sun would appear,

and later the moon, again and again,

here and there, like playing hide

and seek. Or did the music of the

flutes bring us All together.

between here in there

Walkin on a foot path

paved with golden flowers

each one placed there ever so

gently by an unseen

hand of the wind,

every tree is alive

with new leaves in full bloom

it must be springtime

there is so much beauty out

here on a hill side in the

middle of no where. If one was

to write about it, who would

belive.

Solo Sail

To sail around the earth in a solo sloop,

My brother takes to the water.

Sitting on a rock in the stream,

I sail with him on a journey home.

There we go flyin with a fair wind

Dancein across waves of light

Makin music at the tiller.

Soul Sound

There is music in the Soul

Sounds the Most High does

Control.

Withdraw your outer attention.

Come visit within, to a place

Where there is no sin.

Barriers Borders in Boundries

All exist to separate us.

Though many of them are not

physical structures, they are as

effective if not more so, than

a Wall built of stone or steel.

In the maze of our minds,

they can be found, reachin

to the sky and blindin our

eyes. Until we break down

those mental constructions,

they will be the cause of

our distruction.

Moon in the full moon

laying in the grass

watching light dance

on the water,

A clear day seein clouds

disappear, got a lot done

doing nothing.

A river broke a dam. It needed

to be free. The river now flows

full force on a journey to the

sea.

Light in Sound Breathin

light in Sound dancin all

around Breath in the rainbow

Breathe in the Sound, you are

the rain bow, you are the

Sound dancin all around

---

on a clear day

Watchin clouds you can
get a lot done doin no ting

On a clear day
Watchin clouds you can
get a lot done while
you seem to do nothing

No thing

inner Drum

Radient light in sound

a Vibrant celestial music

Showers of grace Stream

Within, all is the Most High

thunderin

over the heavens with a

Ringin Radiance.

℮

Sun Aura

Magical Mist in the air

Most High knows where

Colors go when they seem

to disappear.

All within be still and

See.

your Season is in

To eat and injoy bland food,

use the seasonin of your inner

being. Sprinkle freely according

to taste, and the food of life will be

pleasant. Offer up the blessin

to god all mighty, and the

Spirit Within will be pleased.

Bright shining eyes with moon

in stars there in.

The love and understandin

of God Allmighty is in

us. We can freely give,

for give, and for get.

Tree Love

Have you ever seen
a tree that stopped your
mind.

With leaves branches
flowers in fruit growin
every which way you look

Roots dancin in the air
Birds buildin their nest
among them.

Musgicans
Prayers on instruments

Shall be there at the
Marriage feast of the
anointed, When the
Saints go Marchin in

Makin a joyfull
Sound givin thanks
in praise to the Most
High Master of
our days

Wear in Robes of
light in Sound
flyin on a stream of
Celestial Music

eye  I

Moon light reflectin on eye
joyus tears of love Most High,
eye cry.

To be in harmony with law
Divine is a constant prayer
of mind.

let's get High!

Do you find your self
trying to get high from day to
day and you don't know why?

All over this eart the pursuit
is the same, different substances
different names.

Through many things used we can
be deceived, but in the Most High
we will be received.

So let's get high on the Most High
to be one with god is the reason
Why, We get high.

Fisher of Men

One, man, in a boundless boat of light
in sound, pull in a net, of Naam.

Birds of all types to be seen
on these I slands circle overhead.

He take in the boat, men
women in children of all types
and colours to be seen on these islands,

All way up, over the rainbow,
to home of eternal sunrise.

> Sail on light in sound
> Sail on fisher of men.

Glory Be

To The Most High Praise
his holy Name.

Which one?

The same one
The All Mighty
Glory be

Rain in Town

Walkin through town in

The rain I am fascinated

by the range of changin

Colours to be seen

in the spots of oil

in water, on the road.

IN ONE

A Feast prepared in the pure

land of light on the banks

of a swift Mountain stream

in the mist of a roarin

water fall nectar of life,

eternal gift of love, true

grace divine

Thank God for trees

All life times on this

earth, trees have been lookin

over me. I appreciate the opportunity

to look out for trees.

Grassy Sea

Sail in on a Sea of grass
upon a windswept hilltop

Shadow of a soarin hawk
rides the waves of blades

Sunlight sparkles silver on the
blue green sea and golden sand

grass dancin to Music
of the Wind, I hear surf
in its shimmerin song sound

ONE Divinity

In simple everyday things
see the workin of one
divinity.

In doin all things, keep Mind
in heart devoted in remembrance
of the one DIVINE

All is ONE

The I llusion is that we
ever left home an (or) went away
to rome.

The Illusion is that
there is you or me.

The truth is, all is one in the one.

I am Home

Hey death you can't touch
me now.

I've Met the Master,
I've takin a vow (bow).

To me you've lost your sting.

That's why I sit an sing
you can't touch me now.

I am home where
ever I am. I am.

                    Song
          Night
                    Sound

          In The Stillness crickets can

                    Be heard.

          Amidst Moon in starlight

          Dancin fireflies and night

          Breezes, Wind chimes

          Sing in the trees

─────────────────────────────────────

                    INografi(e)

High Valli

Crickets in the tall grass

Singin strong

All day and night

Sunset on the reef

A chain of islands

Have appeared where

None were moments before.

I considered to journey there

And climb some mountains I saw

Then realized

They were clouds.

60

AllONE

Are we Alone

Or

Are We AllONE

Bamboo

Bam boo Boo bam

Bam boo Boo bam

Bam boo Boo bam

Tam boo Bam boo

OOb Mab OOb Mab

What A Whirl

On the road again, seem to be headin west,

Keep on goin will reach the east,

As long as the road holds out.

A mersades, an some unrecognizeable

Dime store sub compact, pass me buy

In a cloud of dust.

Opposite ends of the drivein spectrum,

And here I/eye am walkin. What a world.

Heaven Hi

No one seems to know why

The popular greetin says Hello

Instead of Heaven Hi

We all know Hell is lo

And no one really wants to go

Yet each time we meet we repeat

Hell low. Why not Heaven High.

Sit in in Silence

What a joy to climb the mountain

After swimin in the sea,

To wade in rivers in streams,

See crystal clear rain come down

In showers of light in flower colours

In sunset in sunrise.

CHE OM RA

CHE took off on a sunny windi day.

Birds in trees were singin,

Bells in chimes were ringin,

As if they knew a friend

Was goin away, that day,

To sit in silence where he can't

Be seen.

CHE
OM
RA

RA
OM
CHE

When The Time Comes

All the time my soul holds on, to this bodi

That needs Nature's sustenance,

Until its work is done.

When that time comes

I want to be ready to let go, in go.

Here I am to serve the one in All

Until our lord calls my sovereign soul home.

Accident Free Life

Remember accidents do not happen
though our life seem to be at the whim
of chance.

The underliein cause of all sufferin is the effects of our
own thoughts words and deeds.

Make it Right

This world is full of so many good

    Religious people

That's why things are, the way they are.

Be-livers who do not live what they be-live,

Preachers who do not practice what they preach,

Like a recipe that has all the right ingredients

In correct proportion, yet comes out tastin

    Terrible

Because the ingredients are not what they seem

    To be

We know what's wrong. We can make it right.

Life

Life is a learnin experience

We have to live and learn

To be one with God we yearn

We learn or burn, We burn and learn.

In memory of the Saints prophets

And sages

That have come down from God

Through the ages,

Teachin mankind in stages,

All for love not wages.

I Call Upon Thee

Master thou art free.

I call upon thee

To save my soul

From the illusion

Of the world.

The glory of God

Is manifest within thee.

There is nothing you cannot do.

If Not for You

If not for you

Things thought of would not have been

If not for you

Things said would not have been

If not for you

Things done would not have been

Thank you

SunRise in the Rain forest

I awake to see sunlight streamin

True the trees,

Reflectin off Raindrops, shimmerin

In every color,

Like millions of sparklein jewels. What a

Treasure, right out in the open.

And I am watchin it.

Truth in ONE

Knowin the truth, a man finds himself

AllONE.

Not understandin truth,

Many others think him alone.

What do you think. Him.

All in All

I am in All

All is in I/eye

See All in ONE self

Know All is ONE, in ONE

A Letter

VIVA Vini

Greetings of life to you, Brother. May the grace of the Allmighty be with you, Allways. I hope this little letter reaches you in the Wholeness of health in mind body an soul. I told Hope Hill that you had to fly on short notice, so you were unable to come up this time and next time God willin you will.

Who looks to see the flowers bloom, or birds build their nest and spiders their webs. One who is in the moment, that is Who. Sometimes it might be you. So watch what you are doin while you are doin it. And be where you are while you are there.

If my stomach is upset, I change my physical diet. If my mind is upset, I change my mental diet, of what I look at, listen to, or read. If you ever find yourself in a similar situation the same might work for you.

Much bad news can be depressin. Especially when their is little you can do about it. Except turn off the radio or t.v. and put down the news papers. Quiet time.
So take time out for time in. Sit still. Become aware of your breathin. By controlin the breath you can control and quiet the mind.

> If not for you
> Many peaceful thoughts would not have been.
> If not for you
> Many plesant words would not have been.
> If not for you
> Many good deeds would not have been.
> By the grace of God it has been.

> Thank you
> Senya

P. S.
Watch your self put on your shoes.

74

II. Travelogue

May 21st 87

With sounds of rain forest reverbaratin within, through the window
I/eye notice five white birds flyin west, as the metal bird we are in
taxi for take off.
In flight there is nowhere we can go that is beyound the grace rays
of love. Even up here above the clouds, I feel the suttle touch of
love's infinite hand.

Flyin over the murki sea surroundin N.Y. City and Islands, seein
the dirty difference in the water, glydin over a sea of airplanes to a
bumpy landin, touch down.
In a crowded city with so many homeless, it's difficult to find a
place to rest.
Many phone calls later John takes us in, his bachelor apt. on 2nd
Ave. an 83 St. shared with maps books magazines and his self-
assembled t.v.'s, on the 26th floor, six floors below the top.

22nd May

Above the din of trrafic sparrows can be heard. Marty is an
excellent travelin companion, introducein me to the trees an birds of
his childhood. Cardinal, one in south Central Park landin twice on
an ancient rock observin us, then dissapearin among the trees.
Starlins grackles and robins sourround us.

Anett in Kimani meet us at 72nd an 5th. Voices of children in the
playground and the roar of traffic engulfes us.
We sit an watch the children play as we speak of past present in
future playin the flutes in spaces where there is one sound.
Marty takes a short nap on a playground bench still digestin the
blueberri and corn muffins we had at breakfast with Jill, Clara's
mother.

As we ride the bus to visit Rashidah, I reflect on a vision in the
subway. Through the grimy window a sign says Bliss St., but all
the faces that flash by look unhappi.
City livin takes the joy out of allmost every one.

In the park, adult Asians picnic an play leap frog, while two
squrrells look and listen to bamboo flute sounds.

In this seeminly hostile enviroment, we feel secure because the god
we know is where ever we are and in all our sisters in brothers even
though they know it not.

Sycamores elms birches oaks maples, lindens, ginkos, and much more, beautiful trees, I cherish the company of their majestic presence lookin over us all.

In Ny York we read at Outrigger pub, the Centerfold, a place for the arts in a church, and the A. B. C. Rio, all on Manhattan. In Brooklyn we read at the Brooklyn Underground.

Speakin with Chanti in Baba on telephone, for the first time hearin each other's voice, yet to me all sounds an feelins are so familiar.

Ridein the subway to an from cumunity radio station WBAI, I recognize all the faces I see though we have never met before.

Havin the feelin that I've viewed this life's movie over and over again, but it's so great I enjoy the reruns, even though some of the scenes are only almost live.

A large flight of piegons perhaps 100 or more move as one undulatin wave of wings, flyin in spaces above the street, between sky scrapers.

In the park I can hear sounds of leaves on trees dancin in the breeze mingled with voices of birds and people speakin in various languages: broken English Spanish an Chinese.

The new moon smilin in spaces between tall buildins, still look the same, as we ride the bus goin to a poetry readin flashin true the neon night.

All along the street in entrances to subway or port authority, it's like enterin some ones bedroom. There are people liein down asleep everywhere.

Some sit up half alert surrounded by all the things they possess.

Anett see us off as we take the bus to Bethlehelm. The iron tonic she just made an gave to us is half finished by the time we get on board.

Before leavein N.Y. Shitty we call Rashidah an say a farewell by flute on her answerin service. Daoud makes the connection.

There is so much I can say, but I won't.
What little I do say will have to suffice.

I try my best to avoid the social constipation that seems to be the ruin of almost every nation.

The beauty of the souls I've met canot be described, but all who know themselves know what I feel.

Through the window of the bus comunities of free flowers still see us and smile, as we seem to flash by.

Seein Seven hawks dancin in circles above, while ridin the bus, this thought comes to mind.

True the grace of the Allmighty we have been alive forever, and there is nothing we can do to not live forevermore. We are in this body for a time, and to leave it is no crime.

So when the time has come to offer up our last attachment, don't cry. Sing and dance one more time.
This is something we have done over and over again, so life and aparent death becomes familiar.

On arrivin in South Bethlehelm the bus makes a schuduled stop a few miles from the stop we are to come off at, so we sit on the bus, Marty readin, I writin in this travel log.
Just then a familiar voice outside says, Want to get off here? It's Marty's farther. Longin to see his wanderin son, he has traveled to this stop on the way, to meet us with joy. We grab our bags, get in his car, givin greetins to each other while following at a liesurely pace behind the bus we were ridin on.
We meet Barbara. She prepares food. We eat an relate experiences. Her daughter Joan visits. We enjoy meetin also Barbara's son David. We visit with him.

In the city of brotherly love we feel sisterly love also. Kim in Terri rejoice to know we have arrived. Receivein directions on telephone, we go to where their families garther.
We pray on instruments praisein Most High, for each others presence. Renewin our acqaintance an meetin the children that were born since we last saw each other. Atu and Bob, husbands to the sisters and lovin fathers to their children, welcome us also, all joy.

On same day we arrive in Philly, we do poetry at open readin held at place called Bacanall. We are well received.

Day after next, poet Ashack and Senya are featured readers. We pray on instruments and do oral poetry. Everyone is joyous. One love prevails.

Day after next, Carolann in Marty featured readers at Nexus Art gallery. Sweet sounds of earth harp, brimbau, mbirra shackers in bambu flutes, ring with radience. David reads some sonetts to everyones enjoyment.

Stayin with Bob in Kim in famili, peacefull meditations in the cellar, light in sound inside in out. I seem to be leavin there. Embraces in kisses are exchanged.

Marty comes for me from Bethlehelm. We return there together. Don in Barbara greet us. We visit where they work at Lehigh University.

Poetry readin at Godfree Daniel's: Carollann is mistress of Ceremonys. In one poem I hear all, in all I hear one.

On the road again drivein through Pennslyvania, we stop to take a leak. I pick daisies for my Mother. It has been five years since I gave her flowers. It's so good to see My Mother in Father Sisters Nephews an Neices.

With Marty at the helm we cruise true the Capitol city like a sunday afternoon drive. Seein hearin companion souls that emerged from the same womb once again is truly a blessin.
Jumpin so high with joy, Marty is afraid my sisters will go true the roof. Somehow they manage not to.

Who can write all that is said?
God talks too fast.
There is so much poetry everywhere, we can't write it all down.

We see the foot prints of a dove in flight. It seems hard to belive such an impression could be left on thin air.
Big rain come lightenin in thunder on the beat box Ricki Rockin with the rythym of life.

Feelin everything all at once through everyone, goin on a trip yet never leavin anywhere, I am right there in you. Why are you lookin all over for me.

Lookin at a picture we/I/eye see all the pictures that were never taken, just because there was no one there with a camera, award winnin photographs each an every one.

It's so easy to write nothing, we/I enjoy doin it, finally findin a way to share the silence, eye rejoice.

A fallin Mango splits the Bamboo flute Shakuhachi is the sound it makes.

Suddenly the barriers melt. There is no me there is no you. All that exzist is the light in sound, within the relentless waves of humanity.

Crashin against the illusive shores of reality, disembodied Voices Talkin, laughin, cryin, rejoicein, All in one breath.

When is the last time we were quiet enough to hear the sound of all our hearts beatin.

Marty an I ride along with my sister Vera drivin, her car followin my father on a Sunday trip into the Virginia Country side. My sister Margaret an her daughter Lisa ride with in my farther's car, to a place called Indian lakes. At the check point there are two Plastic non rust Indians the only ones we see. It's hard to belive we are on land where many groups of these people once lived. All I see now are Billboard Ads where we can visit their sacred burial sites for a reasonable price, or go to resavations controlled by non Indians, and gawk at the remnants of a Nation, while they try to adapt to oppression an survive.

In the capital city we ride the subway goin to D.C. University radio station [WDCU].
We tape record a program that will be aired two days after we leave. On the day before we depart, we tape record another program at Community radio station W.P.F.W..
At D.C.U., program host Ethelbert Miller is pleased with our poetry. Being a poet himself, he knows the feelin.
Grace Cavalieri, program host at W.P.F.W., also enjoy the blend of music and poetry.

The night before we leave Washington, D.C., we visit Lenni at a place where he is house sittin. We enjoy each other's company in a beautiful garden.
At sunset we drive true rock creek Park, on our way to his parent's house. There we meet his mother in father.
After leavein there we visit Leito where he works at Hex Co..

81

When we arrive, he has just got off from work and is waitin for a friend to pick him up. So we do. He is happy to see us all, especially Marty who was one of his school teachers on St. Croix. Together we visit my sister Vera. We get there before she comes home. Marty spreads a blanket on the hillside. We sit and talk. Vera arrives. Food an conversation continue, till early mornin. We say goodbye an drive off to seek some rest in the light of the wanin moon.

> On the road to the Village of the beautiful one
> The hills all over are covered with clover.
> Clouds with happy faces frolic across the sky.
> Fields of purple thistles attract dancein butterflys.

Drivein true pennslyvania dutch Country, seein the farms an the people in horse drawn carriges, so many layers of life on the same plate.
We go off the beaten path to buy raw goat milk from a shy little girl, about 8 years old.
Fresh organically grown Vegitables at a road side stand: We buy a bag full, from a pleseant young girl about twelve years old.

In Bethlehelm again, we innercersize along the river bank, jog, walk in talk. In the water, we see a snapin turtle come up to breathe, then dissapear in the murki depths.
Polution is obvious as we observe direct discharges at the Bethlehelm steel factory. Yet still cray fish, musk rat mother with young, forage in the shallows, tryin to adapt an survive.
Three friends, two men an a young dog, splash about seekin crayfish, havin allready caught a dozen or so. Their rods an lines are baited ready to catch even bigger fish. Pausein momentarily from whistlein an flute playin, we greet each other, sit an talk for a while.
We say so much, once again I must say I can't write it all down.
Yet still blessed with good memory, in the right time an place I will tell it all to you.

We leave Bethlehelm goin to Norfolk Connecticut. On the way we pass true Millbrook New York, stop by to visit Marty's friend Jim, a school teacher who he met on St. Croix. Jim's Mother gives us direct directions. We arrive an greet each other. She is in the precess of movin from this house where she raised her children, livin here for forty years. Now olone, children grown up moved out, husband dead an gone ten years or more, unable to keep up the large house an grounds, she's now movin to a retiament home relucktantly.

We take a short nap in the woods. Jim an his wife Caroll arives. They take us to mill brook school where they both teach. There is a small zoo there. They give us a tour.

We enjoy seein the creatures yet feel sad at their confinement. I play the flute. The music seems to lift their spirits. So much is happenin I can't rite it all down.
I get a feather from a laughin parrot.

On the road again goin to Norfolk Connecticut to visit john our friend who we stayed with in New York.
We arrive in Norfolk get off the main road an drive on an unpaved road into the woods. John's house is at the end of this long windin narrow road, anchored on bedrock among the trees like a mushroom.
John comes out to greet us. We embrace in the night, talk a little, then go to sleep. In the morning he leads us on a hike through some 75 acres of Virgin forest surrondin his house.
We swim in a pond with a beaver house in it, and many blue dragon flies, also a lizard like creature that lives under water.
The mud is very healin. We bathe in it. What a sight to see my friends covered with black mud from head to toe.

We leave Norfolk goin to Sant Bani, Sanbornton New Hamshire. When we arrive, we meet Mark. Together we go to the Meditation hall an Sit in Silence.
We receive some litriture on The Path of the Masters, the life of the Saints. What we read is awesome.
We realize love is contagious. We can't avoid catchin it. Love of the Most High lifts us up, because love is the Master, an The Master is Love.
We leave there with a renewed respect for all life. I feel In spired to apply for Initiation on this path of love.
The importance of a livin Master is Clear, to me.

Mark is at the wheel. I ride with him. Marty follows in the horizon. Through the rain in mist, we drive with lights on. After goin every which way, we hit the right road to Puttmanville.
On arrival we are greeted by Gerri. Her husband Toni is out at the moment. They have designed an built this house, a work of art on the banks of a rushin stream.
They are both initiates of Sant Kirpal Singh, an ascended Master of The Holy Path. Mark is also.

We are to stay here a few days. Durin that time we visit the Kirpal ashram WaWaSiSi. There we meet NiNa, a Mystical Woman of love, wisdom, beauty, whom words canot explain.
Nina leads us on a hike true the surroundin forest, around the rocks across the streams between the trees, pausein from time to time along the way to relate the teachins of the Masters.

Passin by Peterborough we stop to see Regina, a friend Marty met on Saint Croix. She invites us to visit the elementary school where she works. All the teachers are excited by our presence. On short notice they call an assembly of the classes, gartherin the students in the gym. We Make Music recite poetry an tell stories. They all participate and enjoy, the last day of school.

In Brattleborro we visit with Naima, who teaches at Central high, livin in St. croix and Vermont, Publishin her own works and some other poets through the quakein grass press.
Naima has found the time between teachin movin and raisein two daughters, to set up a poetry readin for us at the Common ground resturant in Brattleborro. We are blessed with an appreciative audiaunce who receive us joyously. After the readin we join in a jam session with local musicans. Every one dances.

The morning after the night before eye look happy to behold the simple joy of dancin trees.
Sunny wind blow thank god we still have time to think about nothing.

Thank god Niama has opened her heart an house to us. Together we enjoy many moments.

Collin, a Runner from st croix, comes to Brattleboro. There is a big forth of july 4 mile road race. We all run. Collin places 3rd. We all complete if not compete.

At the school of international trainin, SIT, quakein grass press sponsors poetry readin. An international audiance enjoys beyond words our presence.
After the readin a man from Switzerland mentions his apreciation, sayin allthough he is just learnin english his heart understood every word.
Together we pray for universal love to become a manifest reality.

At first light this mornin we awake and jump into the car, while wipein sleep from our eyes.

We are on the road again before Sunrise. Headlights ablaze, we ride
the hill tops.
Barrellin through fog as thick as clouds, Marty at the wheel singin in
the rusty old horizon.

> We all gonn'a get to the goal
> We keep our eyes on.
> Souls rejoicein just to know
> Love is the Master.
> Safe an sure through grace
> We avoid all disaster.

Next mornin before sunrise we are on the road again movin true
New york. On the way we take a long swim in lake Ontario, then
visit Niagra falls at sunset.
We call Chenzo's sister. Mame is happi we are here, so we eat
custard at her favrite sweet shop, after seein more-than dance at the
art park.
Her children Ben an Christina are away at summer camp. We miss
seein them. After a great breakfast an mornin talk, we prepare to
take off for Ann Harbor Michigan. Just then as we get in the car, a
man ridin a bycycle passes by singin I am on top of a rainbow, not
boastin, just toastin the Most High.

We gasup, check the oil, clean the windshield, flowin with the
traffic, payin the tolls, changein lanes when apropriate, beatin the
rush hour, movin in the fast lane. A loud explosion is heard as a
eighteen wheeler in front us blows a tire.
Pieces of rubber fly through the air. We swerve right then left. The
lanes are blocked. In the nick of time we ease through an invisible
openin.
Narrowly avoidin a close encounter of the final kind.
Fields an farms flash by along with the sound of the wind and
wheels on the road.
Life is a poem. Look you can hear it. Listen you can see it. All
along the interstate there are bits n pieces of truck tires, but that
don't stop the flow.
Because truckers are tougher than tires. These men n women diliver
the goods.

Drivin true OHIO we realize OHIO is Hi in the middle and round on
both ends. So we just keep rollin right along.

We find no suitable place to set up camp, so we push on all the way
through to ann harbour Mich. We arrive at the Olson home on the
banks of a river.

Their daughter Lydie an her husband Chris had arranged a poetry readin for us, but now they are visitin New York, so we miss seein them. Still we enjoy precious moments with Lydie's mother Mary an father Nels.

We jump off the train rail bridge and swim in the river. Hikin through the woods, we come apon a magical field of wild flowers. We drink deep with our eyes and let go, realizein we can't write it all down. So we read poetry that night an split in the mornin, hitin the road with the horizon.

We are on our way to Indiapolis Indiana, where Marty has many friends, havin worked and lived here durin the roarin sixties. Debra Eads, younger sister of his close friend Winne, has arranged a poetry readin for us at the alley cat Lounge.

The readin is well publicized. People fill up the dart room, spill over into the pool room, beyound sight, but still witin the range of sound.

Great Appreciation is shown for our Presence. Poetry books are well received. We get half of the door, and leave there with enough pictures of past presidents to start a Photo Album. But we don't. We trade them in for fruit an juices while on the road again.

Next Stop the ogden dunes on the shore of lake Michigan. There we meet Marty's Aunt Jane an her husband Bill. The renovated round house and added structre where they now live, Has been and continues to be a Summer Vacation spot for relatives in friends on all sides of the families. To be here again fills marty with a rush of Nostalgia.

And though the day is windy and the water rough and cold he still goes for a swim. And later we hike the ogden dunes enjoyin the view with sand in our eyes.

Later that night we drive over to Liberty ville an visit with Tom, Marty's Big Brother. It's good to meet his wife Mary, and see their daughters Deena an Inga again.

Sittin on the shores of lake Michigan, watchin speed boats flash by, listenin to sounds of water lappin on the shore, and unseen toxic chemicals doin their dirty work.

Tom an Marty an I visit their Mother's Mother, Hazel Sheff, in an Imfirmary at 91. It is a joy to meet her. She ask Marty an eye to play the bamboo flutes. We do an she enjoys it sayin with a big smile, "that's something."

Just visitin that Imfirmary and seein the many elders, attendants, an security gards, I/eye feel the pains of agein. It's a blessin for those who can do so gracefully.

Drivein through Gary Indiana the air is thick. Even with the windows up, we smell the stink an Choke on the Polution from steel mills and other factories.
We find it hard to Imagine how people live there every day of their lives. There are so many worlds within worlds, and in some of them people are trapped.

We visit Evanston ill, where marty had an opportunity to grow up. He an Tom show me the school they attended and the trees they knew since childhood.
It's a joy to see them enter the house where they once lived as a famili, only their mother lives their now. I see many of the things they are fimiliar with, some of them made with their own hands. Memories hold us all so close it's difficult to get away.

We read Poetry at an art gallery place called Holsom Roc. The poeple there are very soportive. They offer to make our books available there and ask us to stay around a while.

Next day we go to O'Hare's Airport to meet Marty's mother. Somehow just before take off her flight # is changed, arrivin at a different gate. We look all over for each other in vain, waitin four hours. While we are inside, she is outside. After pagein her twice we leave. She goes back into the buildin, pages us, and waits.
On our way to her house we stop by the Green Mill Lounge where poetry is in progress. We enter an read a few poems. The applause sounds like thunder. Everyone seems inspired to come to us, shake our hands, and thank us for the poetry. When we try to leave we are stopped by people who want to talk with us somemore.
We arrive at the house just in time. Marty's Mother is glad to see us Whole an in good health. Not knowin what had happened, she was just about to call the Police.

All is well. Love without end flows from every heart miind in soul. At the Unity Buildin, we attend a Course in Miracles with Lola, Marty's Mother.

The Circle of Seven is complete. We are everyday people who look just like people who pass each other on the street without givin the time of day. But here we are, sitin, talkin heart to heart.

Wherever we are, in every town or city, we see worlds within worlds, drivin true the poor part of town, and then the rich side of town, seein who lives where and why, who has what an who aint got.

I enjoy the ringin sound of Cicadas. This locust like insect emerges every [17] years or so. From Maryland all the way across the country we hear them. Some places just a few, and in other areas they are all over the road being crushed by the wheels that roll by.

John Olson, Lydie's brother, has arranged for us to read at St. Michaels Juice bar an soda fountain in Millwakee, so we drive there an visit with them on the day of the readin. He is also a writer. His wife [Julia] is a lawyer workin in the interest of abused children. At the readin there are few people but much appriciation.
A tree Sergon who was there discribes us as two points of light appearin as oppersite in colour yet beamin the same love an life.

While in Chicago, we visited North [-eastern] University radio station WZRD, to do music an poetry for an hour or less interview. While on the air the anouncer, Clay, testifies to havin had a nerevous twich in his eye for a week or more; and it just stopped while we were playin flute wistlein chantin with kilimba music, poetry in all; sayin that he had been expreiencein some emotional an mental stress studyin for exzams, while not being able to play his drums, due to neighbors complaining.
Clay felt that what we are doing helped heal him up, and if we had the time to continue doin it for the next three hours of this show because it could only help his listeners. So we did.

And continue to do so where ever we are to this moment, thrue the grace of the all mighty one divinity.
We see an realize that wherever we go people are tryin to work out personality problems, an chracter defects, so they can be whole again and receptive to soular harmonic.

We leave Evanston ill, goin to Misouri. Miles in Miles in Miles of road lie before an behind us movin thru the flat lands, farms of corn as far as the eye could see.
As we cross the bridge over the [Mississippi] river we see the big Arch, an a huge Orange ball glowin on the horizon wink at us between buildings. Once again it's twilight time.

Hedin west we stop in the subblurb of St. Peter for a onenight's visit, with Marty's Cousin Bob, who is not home right now, but due in the next day.

Bob's famili welcome us, his wife Pat and their children Heidi, Becky, Jared, an Jessica. We make Music an enjoy each other presence.

In the mornin we go the the airport to meet bob. Together we laugh an eat watermelon. Before you know, it's time to go. Bob escorts us on his motorcycle. We pass by the car factory where he works. He points to our exzit. We honk horns, and embrace each other with a smile.

Seein Marty embrace his own being in relatives in friends is like Seein Mountains that live in different lands somehow come together an embrace themselves in each other.

Big Sky Country

Passin true the Big Sky country
We see Men in women who block the horizon.
Passin true the Big Sky country
We see true Women in men to the horizon.
Passin true the big sky country
We see Men in Women who are the horizon.

Seein Myself everywhere I go,
eye realize I stay everywhere eye seem to leave.
When I get where I think I am goin,
eye see I am there all the time.

Passin true rocki Mountain country
We see Men in Women who block the Mountain.
Passin true big Mountain Country
We see true Women in men to the Mountains.
Passin true big Rocki Mountain country
We see Men in women who are the Mountains.

Drivin true Kansas Coldorado Utah, all names yet I can't tell where one place ends or another begins, except for the welcome signs.

In Canyon City we visit Greeg, Marty's Cosin, a man who turns the earth into cups bowls plates vases, you name it, he can make it. Right now Greg is movin the works, so we put things in boxes an move them to an fro, while talk in about everything under the son an some that are above. The main character in the movie of life We realize as love.

In the outskirts of kansas city, we visit Dave a friend who use to live on st. croix. He welcomes us expressin joy of our being there. With love for him we say it couldn't happen without you. We prepare a meal an eat together, enjoyin one in others Presence. We comunicate without words realizin we all face one reality: To be in conscious contact with all life, we must maintain constant contact with the One Divinity Within.

On the road again, we see A Stark Mountain robed with misty clouds rollin down its sides. Travelin between Mountains in Valleys of rollin hills, some lush farm land irrgated here in there, fields of wheat; stacks of hay, various shapes in sizes make patterns of shadows. Drivin true Miles in Miles in Miles of bleached bone dry earth littered with stunted shrubs an sparse tufts of grass. Where there are more people eye see less trees.

Waves upon waves of rock, hills in mountains windblown sand ripplein like water, an optical illusion of forms movin constantly yet appearin still. All so familiar, can't tell the difference between what was seen yesterday, or today, a moment ago, or right now.

For a while we get an idea of what the earth would look like without trees. Where there are no trees I saw no people.

With so many friends in loved ones, it's sometimes difficult to keep my mind where my body is. Here I am thinking of you right now.

While on this life's journey eye realize that outer pollution is obvious even to the blind. But it's the inner pollution that goes unoticed. Yet it must be cleaned up. We can't go home with it.

In Seattle, another one of Marty's old stompin grounds, we go to the Magenta red castle to visit Winne who is not at home. So we walk to the park to lie in wait, Marty flat out on a bench, eye liein on the damp grass. We wait asleep for a hour or so. Suddenly we awake to a roarin screamin sound as four blue angels make a low pass over the city. How did they know we had arrived.

Walkin down the street a young girl approaches from the oppersite direction, suddenly seein us just seven feet away. She burst into smiles and waves at us, from somewhere deep inside, where we all live. She recognized something suttle in us and was happy to know we are walkin this earth. We pass not knowin if we will ever see each other again face to face.

90

We get back to the Magenta castle an wait in the lounge. Winnie arrives and greets us. Words can't explain the joy eye feel seein such care an concern between people. We talk an walk pickin black berries. Winnie shows us a large fennell plant in flower, growin right beside the sidewalk. The very air we brethe is pregnant with poetry.

Later we visit Debra, one of Marty's friends from Indiana livin here in seattle with her husband Richard an their daughter Emma. We pitch a tent we have been carryin with us for the first time. And they both offer a pup tent to stow our gear. So with the tents up in their back yard, we are set to enjoy a good night's rest.

But before we go to sleep joe Blondo arrives with a pick up truck of bargain price fruits: bananas, grapes, pears, peaches, apples. So we feast on each others presence and talk about the readin joe has set up for us three. We admire the stylish flyer with a vintage photo of Fredriksted.

Time an time again, as eye apreciate this trip, I am thankfull for friends in loved ones who's help made all this possible, thru the grace of the Allmighty love workin through them. Some of the most suttle experiences are difficult to discribe.

All over this land, coast to coast, from sea to shinein sea, we look in vain to see the physical presence of a people who once lived here in great nombers like the many leaves in a forest of trees dancin to the same life of the one great spirit; a people who were humane enough to wellcome refuges from across the big waters, and help them adapt to the rythms of life on this big land. Now the presence of the settlers' offspring is prolific, but the people who where here before them, can hardly be seen except as place names, on inter state signs, and Addvertisments for Motels resturants or campsites, you name it. Seasons come an go yet every day, people speak of laws without foundation, of right an wrong, while nations build bigger an better/badder War Machines, a policy that speaks of distructive Might as right. In the light of all this Confusion the most high has my Vote. Don't get lost in the maze of worlds within worlds.

At the last exzit in Seattle we attend a open mike Music session. The Musical Poetry we offer is well recived. A few people are so moved they offer gifts of gratitude. I tell them their presence is a present to me and they laugh, Sayin eye have a Way with Words.

One body appearin as Many Climbin the Mountain of Darkness into Light of life in Love.
Receivein Musical Messages from the Master of Sound Harmonics, Solar Strings, Solar Winds.
Singin the Song of light Life in Love, One Word in one Heart Ringin with Raydience.

We visit with Ken an Anita, friends of marty. We enjoy seein their Urban garden where so many herbs, vegetables, an flowers trive in close quarters. We walk in the light of a full moon, between trees along a ravine, under an over a bridge.

Planets Stare, an Stars Wink at us. Tonight we see no Ufo, just bats an planes. Marty an eye attend an open mic readin, at a coffe an tea cafe, held by the red sky. We enjoy listen and readin. After that we go to the Sun spots, open air readin, held on a hilltop over lookin the city lights.
We watch the full moon rise and see the people fly a black bird an a white bird all over the hill lit up by candles in decorated bags. We listen to poems an read also. It's quite a spectacle of light an sound.

In the Mornin eye awake to see the dandelions open in full bloom.

Marty an eye go to the Oxford Club, for poetry readin tonight with Joe Blondo. We sit an talk with friends for a hour, waitin for the place to fill up. Joe begins with some of his poems an also relates an exprence he had while on the way here tonight. And with respect to writers of the past he reads some of Jean Toomer's work from a book entitled Cane. He also reads from a book of poets who commited suecide.
Even with background talkin from people at the bar, All who are intrested listen intently. Charles Overall is here payin full attention. He is a friend who lives in seattle. We met one in other on St. Croix when he visited there. Tonight before the readin started, he walked in the door smilin, and told me he just come from Hawihi in time to see the flyer in Monad's store window. We haven't seen each other in two years, nor kept up any outward communication. I did'nt even have his adress. So for us it's a plesant expected Surprise, to be face to face.
To everyone's enjoyment, Marty, Overall an eye, make flute music as one.

Next day we meet his wife Mellisa an their sons Cassa and Carlos. Together we attend another outdoor poetry readin, at a lakeside park. The moment is magical from before sunset until Moon rise. All the people present are blessed with the joy of One in others presence.

Marty's Cousins Renee an Eric was there with us. They both live with Big Renee an her husband Mike, at who's home we enjoyed our first nite rest an mornin Breakfast in Seattle.
Both renee an erick are writers. At the lake side readin, eric reads a splashin/smashin short story to everyone enjoyment.

On the road again near Bellingham, ken from seattle at the wheel, we stop by a bluff overlookin cloud coverd waters, silloetts of the San Juan Islands mergin with the mist.
At a Park we park the car. Eye walk along a foot path an skip across rocks to the water's edge. It's the first time eye touch salt sea water since leavin st croix.

In Bellingham, we pull up in front of the house where Beth, Bobp, AAron, an Marty live, just as Beth looked out the window. Their famili of four had just returned from visitin California yesterday, where they went to Dizzy land and drove on the free way where they saw signs in car windows sayin sorry I swerved please don't shoot. In their garden we Reap giant Zucchini and Cook a big pot of Many Vegetables stew. We sit an eat, then talk. Eye realize it takes love an all it's virtues to raise a famili.

Joe Blondo hitchhikes from Seattle to Bellinham. Together we leave early in the mornin, drivein to Salmon arm, British Columbia where Marty's father's sister, known affectionately as aunt Wizzie, and her husband Uncle Sig live. Being potters, farmers, artists, loving caretakers of all, keeps em quite occupied.

We arrive in time of Harmonic Convergence. Being moved by galactic beam of love, Aunt Wizzie an Uncle Sig have arranged a poetry readin for us to be held on their farm.
Words can't explain the love we feel being in their presence. At sunsct in the twilight aunt Wizzi lights a box fire on the earth, in the center of a circle of coushions. She sits an tunes her quatro, warmin up the air with a song. Her dog lies at her feet until the thunder rolls. The guests arrive. We sit around the fireside, talk, and recite, under cloudy skies. As rain drops sprinkle, Aunt Wizzi sings a song she wrote called prairie winds. As the clouds blow away, we see stars beamin in the skies.

[Last entry made approximately August 19th 87]

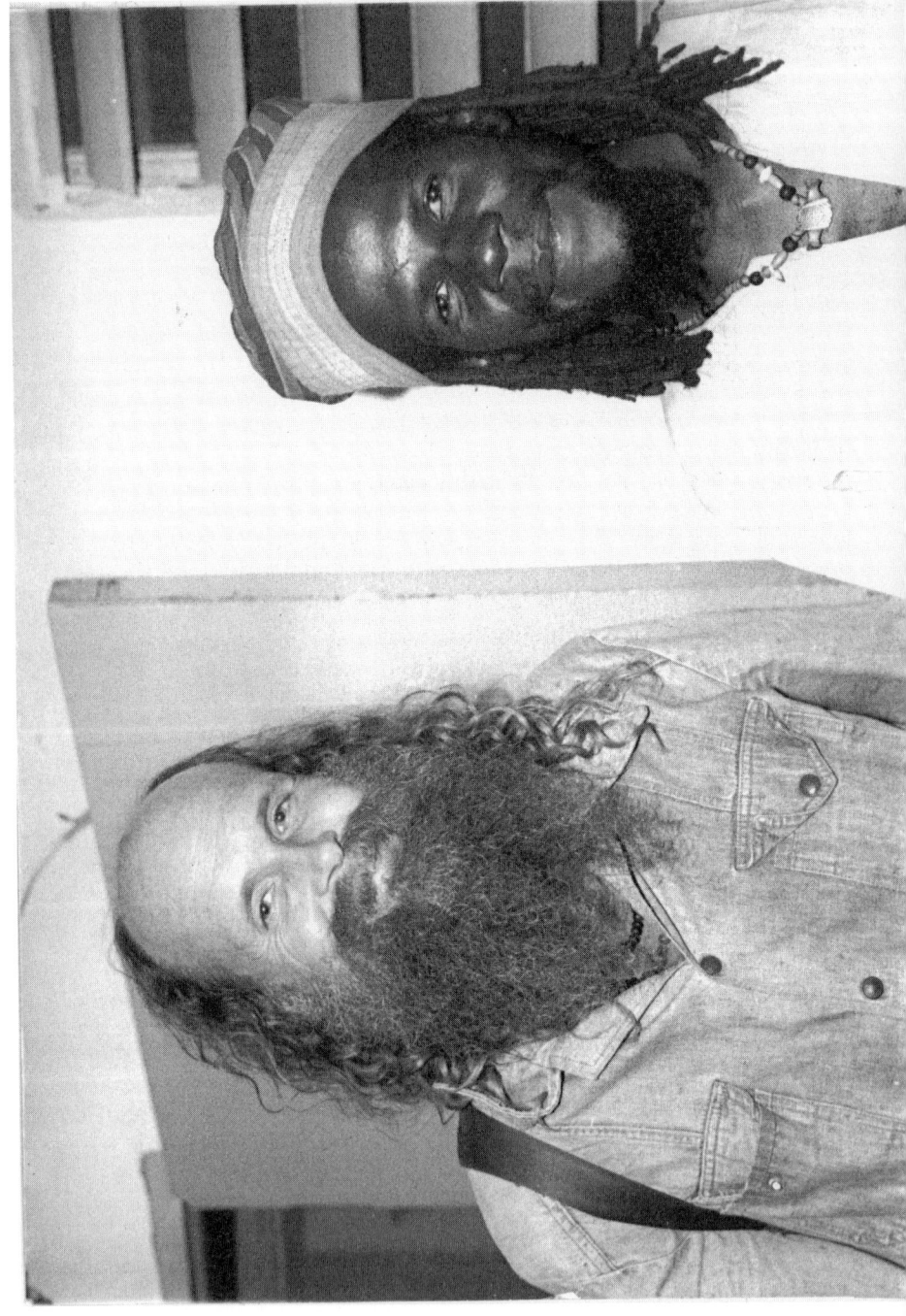

III. Marty's Conclusion to Senya's Travelogue

Marty's Conclusion to Senya's Travelogue

It is an easy day's drive from Aunt Weezie & Uncle Sieg's in British Columbia to the Canadian Rockies in Alberta. As usual, we picked up what hitchhikers we saw and could fit. For this stretch it was college-aged Cassandra and Josh returning to Montreal from their trip out west in their country; the high point, the westernmost, being the forests, mountains, and beaches of Vancouver Island. Across Canada, we gave rides to and met a number of young people making practically the same journey.

We entered Banff National Park in late afternoon, well stocked with corn chips & dip (a trip tradition by now), trail nut mix and raisins, two or three bottles of Welch's grape juice, and perhaps ten 1-liter cartons of assorted juices, from a Safeway at the prior not-so-touristy town of Golden. We were intending to juice fast for several days after the feasting at Weezie & Sieg's, and the trip as a whole, but couldn't resist the 2 food items (Senya the chips, me the nuts).

Our planned several day stay in the Canadian Rockies was in a real way my gift to Senya, and to myself; as I'd been through on this road (Trans-Canada, Rt. 1) a couple times, years before, and they were clearly the most impressive (though not the tallest) mountains I'd ever seen. They are sheer rock. I hadn't had time to stop and hike in them. As a fact, I had hiked in other lovely mountains, and did not feel the need in myself alone to pursue that to any greater extent. Yet I knew (and continue to know to an increasingly greater degree ever since, through discussions with friends and family and re-reading his writings in new light) how deeply Senya loves mountains.

Up until this summer, Senya had never been in what most of us might call real mountains. The mountains his spirit remains forever among on St. Croix are a maximum, I believe, of 1300 ft.. Those of Trinidad I am sure are higher, but likely not half the 9 & 10,000 ft. altitudes common in the Canadian Rockies. In his interim life in the U.S. and travels in the military, Senya did not visit mountains, per se, to the best of my knowledge. Yet he meditated on, sang, chanted, wrote, read, and knew more about mountains than most of us. They have always had a very deep special spiritual meaning to him.

Here we were to enjoy together these mountains for several days, with—for the first time in our 3 month trip together across the continent—no friends or family to visit and no scheduled readings of poetry! We two, on our own time, in our own element, nature.

Cassandra & Josh were so compatably comfortable with us, riding in the car the whole day up into & through increasingly spectacular mountains. I am sure both they and we tried as hard as we might to figure a way we could postpone separation by camping together and hiking together, for we both planned a stay in the national park. But, for personal reasons and bents, they preferred to stay in a hostel as close as possible to Lake Louise, a world famous spot near our western entry to the park. Senya and I had in mind to find a campground near the town of Banff, an hour or 2 further drive, on the east side of the park, and from there to take a 3-day overnight hike into the backcountry. In Lake Louise area, we talked it over and signed up for the hike, while our friends were settling on where to stay. The best hostel for them was already closed for the evening. We drove further, got confused on directions, and finally backtracked to find a second hostel still near Lake Louise, and open.

Now on our way to the Banff area, we passed a campsite that I remembered one warden had recommended. As it was getting late and I was tired from driving, we decided to stop and camp there. It was drizzling and overcast, but not dark yet, probly about 7:30 PM. We saw a female elk and then a male with rather large antlers, lazying through the campgrounds. We played flutes to them and followed them a while. Then we pitched the tent quickly. I was so tired I went right to sleep, rather than help Senya gather pitch from the white pine trunks to take home and burn as frankincense. He had been looking out for a source for a good quantity of this, the whole trip. Here he found it.

That night was very cold, and neither of us were able to get truly warm enough even with the blankets and heavy cotton sleeping bag we had. As came out clearly on our trip, compared with each other, I am a morning person, and Senya a later-in-the-day person. We somehow always managed to indulgently take advantage of this situation rather than make differences. So, I was up and out fairly early and busied myself with a walk around the camping grounds and met again our antlered elk friend. The underbrush was soaking wet. It was off-and-on raining and still completely overcast, so low you could not see the huge rock mountain faces that were all about us. It was not quite the weather we had in mind. It had not been like this at Weezie & Sieg's, and it had not been at all like this when I had passed through before.

Senya was slow to get up, and we weren't sure what to do, but we both had pretty much given up the idea of hiking overnight, so we started to think in terms of day-hikes, returning home each night. It still was dry inside our tent. We talked of leaving the tent to dry where it was, before packing it up and moving it to a campground further east, though it did not look like anything was going to dry for a long time. It was still rainy. I pushed for just heading east with the wet tent in the back seat of the car, while we looked for fairer weather and a nice day-hike. This is what we did.

While we were getting the recommendations of the warden at the camp gate, a wolf with a collar loped by in plain view. She called him by name and said she'd call in to report his sighting, as he hadn't been seen for a very long time. Heading east, now, there were a few breaks where we could see the magnificent mountain we had camped at the base of, and Senya lamented a bit that we could have just hiked up the majestic side of it from where we had camped. It had a sweet green meadow on a steep slope, way up there by its rock face. There was no designated trail here. This was Senya's style—all the more reason to go. But it was still chilly & wet & showing no real sign of clearing. The actual prospect of the wet hike through the bush & forest to get up there was not particularly inviting to either of us. I drove on the slower, winding road (1-A), and we enjoyed what incredible views we could squeek in between clouds, stopping once or twice beside the road.

Now north of Banff, I drove up the switchback road to the Mt. Norquay area, where we had originally planned to start our 3-day hike. This is a major trailhead, and there were several day-hikes we could take from here. It was nearly noon, and though the weather was showing signs of clearing, with patches of blue sky, we made a clear and final decision to only go for a day-hike, and come back and find a campground that night.

This day turned out to be tremendous. We had more rain and a long stretch of muddy path where horse travel made it worse. But the sun came out also, and in a few hours the rain stopped completely. We had incredible, clear views through tall trees up valleys and across at more vast Mother-Nature-chiseled rock mountains. We followed a rushing river, crossed a bridge and went up one of its racing branches. We met only one couple, seeking rain shelter under one of the big trees by the bridge. We followed suit for a while under a tree of our own. It was not a day most day-hikers would hike, but both they and we were very happy we had.

Finally tired of winding our way between hoofprints, I gladly agreed to go up one of the many game trails Senya had been pointing out along the way. This went up much faster, and branched and zigzagged one way and another. Though it was steeper, footing was easy, and we felt so much closer to nature. Still in the trees, noting the wide variety of dung & droppings & footprints, we climbed up and up, gaining altitude surprizingly rapidly. As we rose up the shoulder of our healthy, though lesser, mountain, we looked across the river at the shoulders and peaks of several major mountains. Getting up and up, the expanding view was very exciting. Soon we were above the trees. We headed as much as possible straight up the 45-60 degree incline. Both of us felt very strong, exhilarated, and not at all tired, though I wondered how I would feel the next day. Senya had had good climbing conditioning in the foothill mountains behind Weezie & Sieg's while I'd stayed home & visited.

As compared with Senya, anybody is a clock-watcher, and I was at this point regularly telling Senya how many minutes we had until I felt we should head back. My rule was we should turn around when we had hiked half of the daylight hours, so that in theory we would be out before dark. Senya was willing to go along. Many times I have enjoyed shucking my clock-watching tendencies and going along with Senya's comparative oblivion and just seeing where it led us, always somewhere special. Senya always made out. But this evening I wanted us both to manage a good warm dry sleep. We had a site to find and a tent to pitch.

So, we did head back. And on our way down, a somewhat different way, meeting the original trail at the bridge; we could look back and see that we had come really & truly quite close to the top of the peak we were climbing. We knew it would have been grand. But we both were accepting of my stiff regulations.

Before the treeline, ... while we kept edging over in a meadow, at my insistence, to sit in view of my favorite rock peak while we enjoyed our second liter of juice, ... we met four male bighorn sheep walking up the slope as if it were a Sunday stroll. They seemed to acknowledge us as if we were two more of them, not running into the brush as they could easily have done, but walking slowly through the meadow the long way so as to give us as good a look as possible. We serenaded them with our bamboo flutes.

Further down, we found several scattered bones of a large animal: vertebrae, shoulder bones, and a leg bone or two. After some searching we found a jaw bone, and yes, eventually a 14 point set of antlers. These were of an elk, much like we had seen at the campsite—too heavy, obvious, and illegal (I had quickly consulted my sheaf of tourist leaflets.) for us to carry out, or fit in the car. But we had fun figuring how we'd mount them on the hood & such. Then we, with some difficulty, and at Senya's insistence (moving them also unlawful), mounted them about 8 feet up in a tree, sideways. Our descent was more than fully as grand as our ascent, and the muddy trail out seemed like nothing. It was still daylight when we were looking for a camping ground.

We had been told about two campgrounds slightly east of Banff: Two Jack Lakeside @ $8.50 and Two Jack Main @ $6.50. We headed for the first to check out the recommended lakeside sites. At the entrance gate we saw two huge black ravens foraging around

100

the bush just 6 feet from the car. We had seen ravens along the whole trip across the states, but we had never been near this close. I stopped the car and we watched them for a good while. Then we drove in and found the lake to look artificial, the breeze off it to be cold, and the grounds in general to be crowded. So we went on to Two Jack Main. This one was very large, and underused, so they'd knocked down the price as an incentive. Here we found several areas that were uncrowded, and finally settled on site 11-F, partly because of Senya's feeling for the number.

After putting up the tent, we had juice and more chips and nuts and raisins. We played our flutes a while, as a young couple drove in and set up camp right next to us, in 11-G. Attracted by our music, they invited us over for some hot soup. That nite and the next morning we had nice leisurely visits with them. They are from Austria; she, Hedwig, an elementary teacher who spoke English well; and he, Otto, a snowmobile mechanic, who understood some English, but spoke none. She acted as interpreter in our conversations. That morning, she took what are the last pictures to be taken of Senya.

In between visits, Senya and I slept well and warm, having pulled out extra clothes, coats, and a next blanket I'd forgotten I had. It did not rain, and the new day looked great. This was August 21, 1987.

Only because our neighbors wanted our picture before they left and offered us hot tea with their own fruit syrup from back home, had I even ventured to wake Senya. But once up, leaving sleeping gear in the tent and everything else in the car, we headed for our hike. We managed somehow to fit in 3 grateful hikers, each from a very different part of the world, on our way up the road to the same trailhead as the day before. Two were decked out for 10- & 16-day hikes toward Jasper, and the third for a day-hike like us. The brief ride was visit enough for us to exchange addresses & poetry before setting off in our different directions.

Here, Senya and I had some more snacks, drank a portion of water, and packed our bags with 3 liter cartons of juice for the day. Senya as always took his faded denim shoulder bag full as ever of the handy and expressive items he didn't wish to be caught without: his 3 flutes; his old, handwritten poetry book; his travelogue book of this trip (requested by Olu and steadily kept up to date with a ready felt-tip pen); a handful of his published booklets for anyone we met interested in them; a cassette tape or two of his music and poetry; his bottle of oil for the body, replenished by Weezie; a bandless watch that kept perfect time, which he'd found on the beach in St. Croix and referred to maybe 10 times in three months; personal papers and such. Both of us brought jackets and sweaters.

We each wore pairs of good solid fitting running shoes, given to us by my brother, for our mountain hiking.

In addition, Senya carried a maraca and I a tambourine in our packs. These two instruments were given to Senya by his friend Charles in Seattle to keep a connection through the Harmonic Convergence, of which we were entering the 6th day. I was not as mindful of it then as I am now, but probly what made us settle on the day-hike to the Cascade Amphitheater, out of several options, was Senya's attraction to its reputed indomitable acoustics. We'd been told a famous Canadian pianist had airlifted a piano into this "amphitheater" for an, albeit remote, concert.

The day-hike fellow was going for the same hike. Setting out at about 10:30 or 11, we hiked together the first three-fourths of the way or so, keeping up a good pace and a heated discussion. It never, I would say, got into an argument, but almost magically danced along at the brink. The man was from Australia and saw himself as a progressive, open-minded, liberal thinker, and found himself compatible with only "the most open-minded people of the United States, like those living on Martha's Vineyard." Senya played on this self-conception, as he almost drilled the man with questions about treatment and attitudes towards the Australian aborigines.

I certainly entered the conversation trying to be diplomatic but clearly siding with Senya. The man's belief was that wherever people are, they must start afresh and bare no responsibility for how their ancestors got there, or how they themselves got there. They have perfect rights like anyone else, and must live by the law of the land, he believed. Senya & I were trying to say, perhaps, that if over a few hundred years an indigenous people become a minority in their own land, that those who moved in still owe a primary responsibility and respect to the indigenous minority and their way of life and space.

The man felt that the aborigines of Australia had sadly neglected their own responsibility to themselves. Their leaders had allowed drugs to pervade their society, and most of the youth were serious drug abusers. Then came all the crime that comes with drug abuse. This was not a fault of anyone but themselves he told us. The government & whites in the society had done all they could to help.

When he started to make statements that smacked so to me of racist statements I've heard all my life everywhere in the world I've been, directed at all oppressed people of color, such as "You give them a few-hundred-acres farm, nice housing, and the best equipment, and they let it all go to hell in a few years," well that's when I started to bow out.

102

At times, as always on hikes, paces differed and one or the other of us went on ahead or lingered behind while the other two kept on. Eventually Senya went on and stayed quite steadily ahead. I and the fellow reached a kind of silent truce, agreeing that it hadn't reached argument proportions and such discussions of honest feelings between people were necessary for development of our own thought. Then we came upon Senya soaking in a sunny spot by the path. I stayed with him while the man went on. Later the man hooked up with two younger ladies we had passed several times. We saw them hiking the hogback of Cascade Mountain much later, across from the inner mountain that we ended up climbing.

I mention this discussion only as illustration. Many of us know, and many of us will come to know herein, Senya and his feelings. As positive, upful, and unconditionally loving a man as he was, he felt the pain of life conditions of all his friends, of all peoples including many he had never met, and, I believe, including himself. He felt this deeply & sensitively.

Senya was much taken by the Path of the Living Masters, which several friends of his in St. Croix are on. During this trip we had made a special point of visiting 2 ashrams of this path: Wawasiki, in Worcester, Vermont; and Sant Bani, in Franklin, New Hampshire. Here Senya had applied for initiation by way of the present living master, Sant Ajaib Singh. One of the tenets of this path is that it is one of the faster paths to spiritual growth in this incarnation, to the point that you may not even have to return— unless you wish to help others. Though I hesitate to quote him, I believe he said a number of times that this was no place to live and it was his desire to develop spiritually to the point that he did not have to come back.

I did not know if it was my imagination, but at the time I felt I noticed this discussion with the hiker putting a damper on Senya's inner feelings. This man was so sure of his kindness, generosity, and open-mindedness; and yet was so misguided as to be a pretty hurtful person, by Senya's standards. So sure and so wrong. Pretty hard to have hope in such a world, is what I was thinking.

I also remember feeling that I was so wrapped up in the discussion that I was literally not seeing all the scenery we were passing by! At the point of our reaching the "bowl" of the Cascade Amphitheater all that changed, and whatever shadow the discussion may have set upon our thoughts and feelings was surely erased by the rest of the day. Weather was ideal. A few clouds played teasingly with mountain tops, making them come and go. But it was basically sunny and ideal temperature. We began looking & seeing & enjoying for the rest of the day, together, Senya and I, to a height we had perhaps never reached before.

There was another funny connection that was with us the whole day. Nearly 2 years ago, I began having a mild ringing in the ears, diagnosed as tinnitus. Senya had had the most comforting words for me: "You're in tune with the Most High. You're hearing the One Sound, the Naam." This refers to the sound one hears along with the light seen through proper meditation on the Path of the Living Masters. ["The sound of crickets is a lower sound and is associated with the body. The higher sounds, bells, flute, *etc.* heard in meditation, will calm the mind and pull the soul towards its source."—Kirpal Singh] Mentioned in many Eastern religions, it represents a level of spiritual development and closeness to God.

On this day, from morning and several times throughout our hike, Senya mentioned that he was hearing this sound, too. I believe he heard it continually, all day. Such comments as, "Marty, are you hearing the ringing right now?" "I'm always hearing it, Senya." "Does it sound like crickets?" "It sounds exactly like crickets." "I'm hearing it, too, then. At least I don't think there's any crickets out playing music now." "No, I don't think so." Then later, "I'm still hearing the Naam." "Wow." "It's high, huh?" "Yes. We're in tune together." I do not remember him mentioning hearing such a sound ever before in any of our ramblings together, except in reference to meditation.

The Cascade Amphitheater day-hike goes to a sort of upper canyon between two peaks: to the south, the first, Cascade Peak, which looks out over Banff; and to the north, the second in a several-hundred-mile chain of peaks called the Cascade Range in the Canadian Rockies. We were quite close between the awesome stratified rock face to the south and the steep, rocky slope to the north. There were a meadow and trees and a pond and a stream where we were. Echos abounded with any noise.

We had reached quite fast, it was barely after noon, and we had plenty of day left. The others had started up a narrow path to the shoulder & hogback of Cascade Peak, for the view south over the town Banff. That was not particularly the view we wanted to see.

At the base of every rock face in these mountains there are huge piles of milleniums of eroded, fallen rocks. It is as if they are sorted: One pile is of 12 inch diameter rocks, one pile is of 4 inch diameter rocks, and so on. It is further into this sort of "canyon" and onto these piles of rocks that we hiked. Eventually I thought I could shortcut up the steep rocky side to our left. When I came back to the rock piles, Senya was nowhere to be found. I then looked up, and there he was way up farther on the same steep, rocky side to our left (north). I clambered up and caught up to him. Here again, as yesterday, we were gaining elevation fast.

Both of us were strong & invigorated. I was not feeling any soreness from yesterday's exertion. It was the kind of climbing where you look up and proceed this way or that, and then at some point you turn around to sit down and take a look and rest. For a long stretch we looked directly across at Cascade's rock face, face to face. Our terrain was of semi-solid rock protrusions amidst patches of soil with low forms of plant growth. There was the thrill of risk but no real danger of falling very far. There was the far greater thrill, leaving me just as shaky, of awe at the immensity and vastness. It made you feel very tiny. This escalated with each higher vantage. Senya and I were in a state of joyous reverence. Senya had none of my shakiness. He was relaxed and completely absorbing every moment.

At one point I must have commented on this to him—his sure-footed, fearless, seeming casualness at these heights, in this vastness. I remember him saying, "It is not up to me, it is up to the mountain. Look how we came up. If it had wanted to, this mountain could have gobbled me up several times over already."

From here, our experience and our conversation was truly elevated. Senya said we should have a camera for this. I was saying no camera could take all this in. He said, "But just that picture of you there and that mountain behind you, and the sky. We should have a copy of that to give your father." "Yes, I cannot deny he would love that."

Somewhere in here he muttered something about permission, and that his parents would never allow him to do something like this. "You mean your mother and father would not give you permission to hike up here in the mountains?" I asked. "No," he said. And then he asked, "Would yours?" "Yes they would. I mean my mother would but wouldn't want to hear all about it. And my father would and would thoroughly appreciate and enjoy the thrill of risk and adventure of it. He would want to come along if he could.

"I mean, Senya, my father is the only one else in my life I've ever fully enjoyed swimming with. We would set a goal and swim out to it, and then swim back. Just like you and I do at the submarine buoy or at the Stone Bird [on St. Croix]."

"Wow. There's love. You really have a loving father— giving you that kind of permission." I hesitate to quote, I do not feel my memory is that accurate. I am not even sure "permission" is the word. But these were the gists of our conversation as best I can recall, and they still are very clearly ringing in my ears.

The topic of permission came up again further up. All through this time, we were climbing vigorously, gaining altitude pretty fast, and then sitting a while to rest and chat and take in the view. Each view was grander than the last. We started seeing tiers of mountain peaks behind tiers of mountain peaks. Senya said, "You know, I feel you're the closest friend I have." I just smiled in the sunlight. "Of course it depends on your definition of close," he continued, "Doing this together is my idea of close. Giving each other permission."

Here the air was thinner. We found ourselves breathing hard, and we started taking more frequent rests. At one point I counted 8 tiers of peaks, one behind the other, looking west. We were eye to eye with 9 & 10,000 ft. peaks in all directions, some with snow, all with rock. And then we were on the top of ours: I would say close to 9,000 ft. high. We had come over the spine, or hogback of our mountain, and could now see a whole new panorama of mountains, including the sheer rock face of a next mountain, again, to the north. The mountains immediately to the north and to the south of us appeared to connect to the east of us, like a "U," thus making, perhaps, the true amphitheater. The peak we were on divided this "U" down the middle. Several times during the day we heard the reverberating echos of a random rock falling, somewhere along these faces. You could not tell the location, as the echos rebounded back and forth.

We were not, in truth, on the highest point of our hogback. It got higher to the east & lower to the west. Senya went a little farther east along it and came back, not seeming to feel the need to go to the highest of the highest. And I, who had determined on this day not to call the clock for the clock's sake, but to enjoy and indulge in Senya's sense of time, was now fatigued. I told Senya I felt I should just put energies into going down.

Down the other side, it looked to our eyes quite clearly like a shelf of rock strata angled safely all the way down to the rock piles below, where we could easily walk right out. It appeared much easier than the way we'd come up, so we headed down that way, on the north side.

The scenery was fully as beautiful & majestic. It was 6 o'clock. The sun was still a few hours up. Senya continued to stop and marvel and exclaim at each view, near and far: fossil in the rock, angle of sun on a mountain, cloud in the sky. He was still invigorated and full of energy. I was tired and focusing on getting down to where we could walk again. We talked about this and continued to appreciate each other's condition. At one point, just out of the blue, in a way he'd never done before, Senya said, "I love you, that's all I've ever been trying to say." I took this richly to heart, and understood it to mean that he'd loved me over all the time we've known each other.

106

Then, not 2 hours before he left this plane, there is one sight I will never forget. He didn't need to point it out to me. They were very bold, and as far as I know, rare up here—Two huge ravens circled, part way down into our canyon. Wide lazy circles, with just a clear few of their characteristic cries. I don't remember hearing echos. Senya turned to me with a smile, "Do you suppose those are the same two black birds?" I thought a little, "Yes, I guess they must be."

We continued down. But when we were nearly to the rock piles, we realized our eyes had deceived us. The rock stratum we were on ceased and made a straight vertical drop at this point. Looking down from where I was, I could see shelves below, but no clear way to negotiate from one to the other. Senya rounded a corner that I would never have thought to look around. It looked like it led to sheer cliff. But he said he saw a shelf there that led to a rock pile where you could walk right out.

At this point we could not see each other, though we were less than 20 ft. apart. We were talking easily to each other. He said there was loose rock on the ledge, something we had successfully avoided so far; but he felt he could make it. I reaffirmed that I felt too tired, and thus too weak, to do any climbing more precarious than what we'd been doing. I reminded him that we could always climb back up to the top and find a next way down. He said yes, he knew, but since we'd come all this way it seemed easier to just go ahead here, down one time. Besides, he said, he didn't really feel like going back around that corner he'd just come around.

I was anxious. I wished he were sitting beside me to discuss this. But over the years I have come to greatly respect his judgement and his capabilities and steadiness in precarious situations. I also felt at this point that objection would aggravate the situation. I said that I would wait where I was until he got down, and then I would follow in whatever way he advised. He said O.K.. I said to be careful, and he said he would. There was no anxiety in his voice.

There was quiet for 5 or 10 minutes. Then I heard a small bunch of rocks fall, then another. I heard nothing else. No voice, no cry. I was concerned and did not know what to do. Senya is sensitive and if he knows someone is anxious, he will ease them if he can. I was sure he would tell me something when he could. There was no way he could get out of earshot. If I called out it might distract him. I forced myself to wait 10 minutes by my watch. Silence. I then called out, then yelled, then whistled very loud. Nothing but echos replied. I was dumbfounded.

Something was definitely wrong. Whatever his condition, Senya could not reply. I felt tied. I looked over and down as best I

could from where I could get. I could not see him. I felt there was
no way physically I could climb around that corner. There was no
way for me down. The only hope was to go up and find a next way
down. The sun set with three bands of magenta so wide that they
filled the western sky. When I look back, it is hard not to see it as
the spiritual sunset/rebirthing of the spiritual sunrise Senya speaks
of in his pome, "Magenta Magic."

From here was the most difficult 18 hours of my life; but as
best I know now, Senya's physical life, on this plane, had ended. It
is his belief, expressed many times throughout the trip, that one's
true spirit self never dies: it has always been, is, and will always be
alive.

To Senya, I called out words of comfort, the name of the
Master Ajaib Singh, and the Most High. I said I was coming the
best way I could. Not knowing if or when my mind or my body
would blank out, I watched the time carefully and took notes to
myself and left notes along the way, as I climbed back up. I did not
blank out; and I don't know how, but I hiked up in an hour and a
half, and for another hour and a half along the hogback spine to the
west, all in the dark. It got steadily lower, until it went so far and
steep down that I could not see where it went. I stayed there for 6
hours until it was light enough to see. It was too cold to sleep. I
kept warm by activity; building a rock wall for a windbreak, and
pacing. When I stopped to lie down, I shivered too much from the
cold. I had 1 liter of apple juice, of which I squirted enough from a
small hole to keep my mouth moist, but I saved most of it for
Senya. Every hour throughout I was calling out and whistling for
help, with no response.

The moon rose, a fine crescent, just before the sun: 2 days
before new moon. With dawn, I saw my way and proceeded down.
I rounded the base and looked for Senya. I was confused and
almost gave up, not knowing what to think, when the sun came over
the mountain and showed me exactly where we'd been, by its
shadow. From there I found him. He lay in a tossed position on
his right side, as if he just had fallen, and never moved. I went to
feel his pulse and found his limbs hard like the branch of a tree, and
very cold. His head was on a stone with blood beneath. Though
his face had minor cuts, one could easily see his eternal hint of a
smile ready to bloom. His bag had burst. Flutes, kalimba, and a
tape lay on the rocks, 10 & 20 feet from him. Up above, on a shelf
below the one he'd been on, some pages fluttered. I saw nothing
else and looked no further and picked nothing up. He had fallen
over 60 feet. In my judgement a rock must have given out
underneath him, and he must have "died" instantly.

I talked to Senya for a while. Then I walked out, overwhelmed with emotions, the 3 hours' hike to where the car was. To most people, perhaps, Senya's wishes for his body after his passing are either impossible or impracticable. But to me they are real, and I was faced with a great quandary here at this moment of near complete exhaustion. His wishes were to be left where he lay, not buried, and no one told, particularly his family. He wanted the one who knew to return some time later and make a flute of his thighbone. A number of his dearest friends knew this well, from his word over the last few years. I do not know, but I think this could have been done. I do not regret what I did, but I do continue to love this concept Senya offers us.

Having met Senya's family on this trip and knowing the love that ran between them, I could not not tell them. I called them and they were stricken with grief. I then reported his passing to the park wardens. They recovered his body, which was flown to his family in D.C. and buried nearby in Virginia. The wardens also recovered his two books (published here) from the rock ledge above him. For this I am deeply indebted.

Slowly, carefully, I drove my father's car back to Pennsylvania, seeing both my family and Senya's family on the way. My trip home to St. Croix has been long and hard, and yet strengthening and uplifting. I have survived only on the incredible net-hammock of love outstretched by Senya's family/community, now far and wide.

For me, the end of a trip; the beginning of a Journey—one I hope to continue to see you, the reader, along. I will never cease to see this friend. And I will always ride comforted upon the riches of our spiritual trek together on this earth, which is, as he said, "to work out our personality flaws and character defects."

IV. A Companion of Senya's

by Marty

A Companion of Senya's

My journey with Senya, Senya will tell you—and yours, also (and his with us)—started before we were "born." I include here a sprinkling of journal notes I have written since I've realized it'd begun, this time. Interspersed are a few pomes, essays and whatnot I've written along the way. The order is chronological.

Senya's writings were, I believe, completed before they were written down. I cannot say the same for most of mine. It is my hope that you can endure the pieces and that some of them may find completion within your heart.

— Marty

Journal Notes

9/24/84: Friday I found Senya. Saturday I helped him build a new nice lean-to .... Sunday I woke up under it and went for a long longed for soak at Senya's pool. A good one. In water & sun.

———

3/4/85: Senya: "You have to withdraw with respect & love. Like the sun. You would burn them if you stayed in the same place."

———

7/6/85: What am I trying to say?
I am so distant from what I am trying to say!!!
I must get closer, to what I am trying to say.
My god.
It is simplicity.
It is Senya.
And <u>then</u> to say it!
When I <u>get</u> <u>there</u>, then to say it!
Oh Lahd, How then to say it?

———

7/26/85: When you live under a tree you always have these gifts in the morning or in the afternoon or maybe ... at night (leaves, blossoms, seeds, twigs, and pods). One brushes your side or flutter-lands on the top of your head or your shoulder. A bouquet for the day. What can you say, but cry?

———

A Teacher

It is so obvious. The look on his face, tells all. It is so simple.

There is music behind it. But it is there <u>in</u> the music. If it is there, the music is there.

In a Letter 8/16/85

... [Senya] makes [bamboo flutes] to have sound in accord with
Mother Nature's music, not the Western(?) or any other man's
scale. So you do not play all your favorite songs. You learn to play
another way, where each note is an event, perfect, and each rhythm
is so, and a flutter and a screech, all flow into one, lovely, breath,
imbibed from Mother Nature, along with the birds and the breeze
and rattling seed pods. A way I am just learning just barely
learning. ...

Journal Notes

2/20/86: Everything is in such a hurry.
     And everything is in need of such intricate plan and
attention. Even going on a trip. And fishing (Carlos). And any
job. Children. And yourself. One of them alone would be enough
& plenty.
     Resolution of conflict is seen to be the substance of all
writing. And all life. I do not & can not live on that level.
     All of that is wrong. You can make mistakes and relaxedly
go on through life. Eyes open for joy. And learning, piece by
piece, from these eyes & these mistakes, & these movements, just
as a Tai Chi master, from slow motion, learns to dart like a cat. And
Senya.

2/26/86: So (yesterday) Senya comes over, rather early talkin about
presidents & showin some joking agitation further along at that I
don't make any signs to (lend him some money). He refuses to say
how much. Any amount, he is sure he could use any amount.
What's his is mine, what's mine is his. (What's mine is not his.
What's mine he doesn't want, and often tells me I don't want.) He
plays an edge. And shows/feels remorse when I challenge him on
it. He has also, all along these 2 weeks, been most (patronizingly?)
humble about wanting me (though not very actively helping—as by
hawking or selling to stores) to get back my money spent in getting
his book Rise in Love published. He wants a video. He may be
layin low for that. But, he had to humble to come ask for money. I
put pressure/resistance on 2 fronts, in our dance of discourse: (1)
time (hurry) & (2) money.
     He did seem in a hurry. I bucked him just as he would me.
When we are together, it is timeless. And that is how we would
have it be. He gave in gracefully/generously, or what developed
wouldn't've been able to ensue.

114

On the money, he never eased, keeping the tension, and at the same time feeling the tension. It is real. He sees on many levels. And it is an edge that cuts close to me. But he has chosen and I have chosen. And the relationship is between two very different very same people. There is danger & the light goes on when he refers to rich philanthropists and that he doesn't break in & take. There is the very tense & the very light. I do not believe he wants to ride. And I do not want to give him a ride—to have anybody riding. If he wants to exist without money, then he must really. I can & do lend him $5 a month, say. But if it gets to more than that, then he is riding and kidding himself as well as others.

When I pressed on the money—how much, how often, to what extent is what is mine yours, both of us in our serious joking mode, me consciously matching & calling his—he said (as if changing the subject), "Write more pomes, happy pomes, ... not like mine[!]" (I have been selling his on the point that they are positive, upfull.) He went off for a while on this. And I said, "Why did you say that?" "Say what? Did I say something?" "That's what I figured," I said. He seemed to really slump into a sadness. (He is perhaps an incredible talker, a controller, who can't take flack. Yet his needs are so very little. Needing little is another very effective tactic, in his existence.)

The conclusion of this entry is a combination drawn from my journal notes and a letter to my brother covering the same topic.

We got to talking about how a neighbor of mine does not carry out responsibility in several areas: The neighbor has two hauntingly thin (skeleton) dogs, through lack of care & feeding. The neighbor's children take part in absolutely no consistent or substantial schooling (3R's) of any kind (though there are sputters), going on 2 years, now. ...

I said I didn't know what to say, because it couldn't be heard. It was a shut out. Too much to deal with, so blinders-focus. Aperture set in. Too much light. And by my very presence I am saying something. Even that is sometimes spoken to.

And then Senya said it may have something too to do with past relationships & numbers of relationships. [There are a prior marriage and prior children.] We both literally jumped upon that. Dropping all jokes. Both Senya & I feel we sense something deep in my neighbor's despondency (my favorite word, these days, in looking at the world and myself) that is very reminiscent of both of our own experiences with respect to energies & completion levels. There is a kind of a dragging, dimming, and empty stomach feeling that comes and goes (perhaps never outgrown), that lingers from past relationships. This is something Senya & I feel even though neither of us has own-blood children.

For me, it includes three persons who are still friends. So I am speaking not only of relationships that are past and done, but perhaps more of past-more-deeply-than-present relationships. I am not saying that I would go back and change anything. I do not regret the breaks under the circumstances. I do not regret the relationships. But past relationships do affect my approach or lack of approach to any future arrangement of relationship.

Senya said that even as he was walking down the road this morning, he was looking at himself saying, "What am I, to be looking like this: eyes half shut, drooping down cheeks, frowning forehead?"

Both of us were realizing we were not in the fullness of our essence. But felt still in touch. Sometimes just marking time. And in writing, that is fine or better. We are there & might get that across. And we are not writing to Messiahs, afterall.

It was about down but it was an upness conversation, if I ever had one.

So out of perhaps high friction came deep connection. But I feel we have yet (perhaps a human condition) a lot to work on.

We said a lot more: fighting over who was whose elder; preparing the upcoming reading at length, and it was truly nice & ready.

In Senya there is a tightness and a daring.

In a Letter 3/10/86

...

I mentioned to you Senya, my poet- or more nearly prophet-friend. Enclosed is his promised book, Rise in Love, three weeks off the press. Some friends of mine have deeply loved his recording/readings over the radio. But I still feel that neither recording nor printed page come close to what he is on a personal one-to-one presence with each of us. His incessant capacity for this magical one-to-one presence is, to me, an awe-inspiring genius.

I know many poets on this island whom I would immediately recommend as poets, but only Senya have I come to share and work with as a sibling. With deep mutual appreciation, we feed off of each other's energy, to the point that I can at least say I am a far greater performer with him than I am alone. And so it is that I am suggesting application be made for the two of us to come up together rather than one alone. But either way would be fine. And welcome. And appreciated.

The grant arrangement might be ever the more sacredly apt for Senya, in that he is a man who does not live in any exposure to or use of money, beyond a possible casual maximum of $10.00 a month "lent" for car-fare, non-wild food, or a pair of Chinese blackcloth slippers; and so he would likely never otherwise make a trip to the states to even avail a poetry reading. This above sentence, alone, might stand as his most accurate resume. Senya, dark black locksed, was born & raised in Trinidad, moved to Washington D.C. with his family at 21, did stints in both the navy and marines, worked odd jobs and was active in poetry back in Washington, then moved to St. Croix where he's been 5 years. Living in and upon "the bush," as we say, he, when pressed, will describe himself as a free spirit, not a Rastafarian. Though he writes without dialect, he speaks with a clear enunciate accent, almost formal, certainly musical. He makes & plays bamboo flutes and flows equally comfortably in presence of drums & kalimba or birds & trees. He is 35 years old. When approached in regard to a resume, he insisted the book would suffice for that and refused anything other—the same response he had given the request for an "about the poet" page in the book itself: "If anyone reads through the book and takes it in, they will know as much about me as there is to know." But I don't think he will beat me for adding what I have. For the many ways I have tried to in my way gently translate his way to others (as in secondself-publishing <u>Rise in Love</u>) he has been clearly thankful.
    …

A Brochure Listing 4/86

<u>Rise In Love</u>, by Senya. 14pp., illustrated. $3 US
To use my friend Ben's word, "upful" poetry, in a clear style accessible to all, by a man born & raised in Trinidad; then Washington DC, with stints in both the navy and marines; and now 5 years here on St. Croix, locksed & in nature. A free spirit.
    To nail his oral poetry down to the page is almost impossible, almost cruel, and most necessary in this age. A dear friend, I hold him more near a prophet than a poet. Just the day before yesterday, on our way home from a reading, walking the long way down Centerline Road, he said and he said and he said in every way possible that it all boiled down to 3 things: light and sound, and breathing. We heard the flowers and saw bird calls as we breathed into his own hand-hewn bamboo flutes. A treeman, myself, I noted that most of us feel that trees don't breathe; but indeed, if trees didn't breathe, we wouldn't breathe! Senya.

Green Key

We were kayaking together for the first time. My friend, captaining in the rear, headed us this way and that and eventually on around toward Green Cay.* It drew both of us as a magnet. What was it about an island that is reserved by man's law for no man, for wildlife alone?

The rocky point upon which the silhouette of a pelican payed us no mind. Close-cropped, wind-combed trees-into-bush, -into-rock, -into-sea. As we followed along the many-pocketed outer shore, there was a sudden cute offer of beach.

All the while circling around the cay, my friend extolled his own sensitive restraint from landing: He knew that our desires met, but my style was more to the law. I remained silent.

As we rounded the long corner to the inner shore, three finned pale men rose upon a second stretch of beach. Pulling 3 dry towels out of a ziplocked bag, they spread them selves out in the sun. The five of us nodded, each a slight and hesitant nod, and not in unison. This protected side of the cay was posted with signs, as many and as obvious as trees. Though we couldn't read them, we figured we knew what they said.

The law thus diluted, somewhere along I broke in to the monologue with, "If you did go ashore, I wouldn't exactly not be with you." The boat continued deliberately on around again and knifed up on the first beach, an offer I was somehow surprised to find still extended, and yet found my self jumping out to steady the boat in.

Then, entirely out of my own control, I sat knotted into the smallest position possible right next to the kayak. I was neither frightened nor ashamed. It was a wholely different sensation. Up through the spine and blood fingers inside me loomed the huge sacredness of the sand & rock I sat upon, of the flora, of the fauna, ordained by man to never meet man. Never to be befouled: that was the purpose, sadly, accurate. Whose law was this really, that I honored compulsively with every fiber of my body?

On my own soul, the scar left by boat and feet in the sand was only minor, as I became the tremblingly honored guest of creation untattered, unpaved. Even if the creatures sparred among

------

*Green Cay, an islet off St. Croix, is a national Wildlife Refuge intended to be completely restricted from human presence.

themselves and won and lost, even as they faced high and low seasons, or advanced in what appears to us as folly; this must be let, to allow: this most magical balance of the Most High.

When my friend returned from a swim, it was my turn for monologue:

"Consider the creatures themselves. Why disturb them for our own enlightenment? Even if I am a special person, should I get them into the habit of expecting sensitive people? If they <u>have</u> had a previous encounter with humans, are they likely to take my presence mildly?

"Few among us would intentionally do harm. Yet look at what mankind does as a body. Many mistakes have been made. And there needs to be some sanctuary somewhere—in our hearts and on our planet—for/from all of us.

"We are a spectacle, an example. Like the three men on the other side. It doesn't even matter what we do or how careful we are: We know what we are encouraging."

As we paddled home, I realized with sudden clarity the overwhelming feeling I had had behind it all but could not express: This is exactly in every aspect how I feel living on St. Croix, a white in a black society.

Back at dock, he said still that the creatures should not be kept from a chance to meet such a dear and unique fellow creature as I. Again, we might all rightly say and feel that. It's true. I wait for the day in which we can—approach all other beings as fellow creations of the Most High.

Journal Notes

9/3/86: Senya says: "How little I have in common with all the other people in the world. To them I don't mean nothin. What reason do we have to keep on? It's just love that keeps us goin on doin what we're doin. It's just love. Nothing else."

———

In Senya, belief in reincarnation keeps him alive to get out!!!

———

You could hear his notes flying, from across the hill. It was far enough that the low notes would be fade and then lost. High and then low. Fluttering, perhaps in the wind, or the mind, the spirit. She, the music, was alight. As if on a branch, a flower, or bird of the tree itself, about to give bloom, or is it birth, or is it seed? Featherweight eggshells tumbling on air as if the air were a trampoline or a floor mat, but a very soft one. Tinkling like dead coral tapping coral, but life. Life itself, music. Music that glow. And you see: from just above the belt. You would see her plummet enroute to crash—and then lost—in silence of low note. Imaging the scene, you were delightfully interrupted by ... SENYA

In a Letter 10/14/86

... Ginger Thomas, the colonial (for lack of a better word) flower, is in full bloom: Unquestionable yellow. (My dear friend Senya insists upon saying "gold." To him the term "yellow" does not impart the sacred awe due the color itself.) The whole hill over! Gold.

A Portrait 2/8/87

Senya

He's just like me and he's entirely different. I guess that's how any friend is you know real closely. People have no question as to why we are friends, assume we live together in the same place, and often give us messages to give to the other (even though we may go 2 weeks without seeing each other). And yet there are times in our interplay where we look at each other like we can't either recognize a bone in the other's body, to say nothing of get next to it!

Two thin pegs—or should I say fence rails—we are known to rarely eat meat, but more likely fruit from directly off the trees. We know where to find it, and dally there by preference, our haunts moving with the seasons. He has long—what would be termed dread locks; but he prefers to be called, along with his hair, natural and free. If you refer to him as Rasta, he will correct you immediately. He bears that image, but will point out to you that that image went on long before the origins of the way called Rasta, closer to the origins of humanity itself. And if you have the time to look at him one minute longer, you will come to agree he looks his chosen part, all the more. And you admit to the beauty of it. You find yourself wondering if this wouldn't happen to us all . . . if we let it.

He is very dark. I am quite apparently white, though I have no papers. We are the black and white of it. Opposite sides of the coin. When you hear us, you get the original with the flip side. And at our best, we play on that.

A Dialogue written down 3/7/87

Senya *comes down the road playing bamboo flute.*
Marty *replies in kind, by playing his bamboo flute.*
Senya *plays his flute, and then says*: Yes, Um Hm.
Marty *plays his flute.*
Senya: Um Hm. Yeah. Marty, you've really gotten into this
 writing thing. You're going to get lost, so nobody will find
 you.
Marty: Yes, Senya. I have to confess to that.
Senya: Well I thought it was a perfect day to come down and go for
 a swim.
Marty: Senya, you're more on time than on time. It's even written
 in for today on my calendar.
Senya: Right on target, huh?
Marty: Yes, sir. That's Senya!
Senya: Marty, you know you've got to be careful about taking
 yourself too seriously. This writing. You'll get strength. And
 you know what happens to people who get too much strength!
 ...
Marty: What?
Senya: You know. "What happens?" Think of all the people you
 know in history who've gotten too much strength. There's only
 one way to go.
Marty: Yeah?
Senya: Well, let's go. Put that away, you've done enough, Marty.
Marty: Yes, I have. I'm ready!
Senya: Put that away, and let's go. But first my nutrients are
 lacking. What do you have in the way of nutrients around here?
 Ripe papaya? Ripe sugar apples? Ripe mango?
Marty: Well, Senya, you hit me at a pretty low time for the pantry.
 Let's see. I have a pear, though. Will you just set a minute
 while I make the salid I was just about to make with mostly the
 pear, and some greens? I know you don't like rabbit food.
Senya: No, but I'll just take the pear as it is. That will do me.
Marty: But then I won't have a pear.
Senya: Well I'll have half.
Marty: O.K. Here. Care for a spoon, kind sir? I know you don't
 usually, but. Live it up. As you wish.
Senya: No, thank you. I'll do fine with it as it is.
Marty: O.K.—Oh, and I have tomatoes. I forgot, I have tomatoes
 to offer you.
Senya: That's O.K..
Marty: Oh, you consider that to be rabbit food, too? A tomato?

Senya: No, I'll take one or two, but ...—Um. This pear is not so
good.
Marty: Oh, wow. I'm sorry. It's spoiled.
Senya: Well, it's not so good.
Marty: Yeah, it was the last to ripe. Probly picked too soon. And
it's way out of season this time of year. Sorry bout that.
Senya: It's O.K.
What you need to do to make the salid? How long that
gonna take?
Marty: I was just gonna pack the makins and go.
Senya: Oh, great.

. . .

Marty: Wanna ride bikes?
Senya: No, I like the meditation of walkin. Keep a low profile.
Incognito.
I like to watch the cars whiz by, leavin me in their dust.
Marty: Let's go. Believe it or not, I'm _ready_!
Senya: Things are dry, eh? We didn't get much rain yet, even
though I read that pome about 'The Rain is the Spirit' and it
started to rain when I first read it. The real rain hasn't yet come.
Marty: Yeah, this path is really clear, now.
Senya: Clear and hard, and dusty.
Marty: Ah, God, what a nice day! I never could of guessed this
morning ... how it would open up.
Senya: Right on target every time.
I try my hardest not to have no goal. That is my goal: not to
have a goal. That way which ever way I go, I'm right on target.
Every where, any way, you go is right on target. You can't
miss the bull's eye!
If you focus too much on one goal that's not meant for you,
that doesn't just come along and find you, then you force up too
much strength, and you're gone, lost. That's what happens to
people who get too strong. There's only one way to go. They
fall. They fall down to pieces. After up, there's down.
Marty, really in this life, that's why it's so important to
focus on the word of the Masters. To get the final upliftment
from this plane. So you don't have to come back. To where it's
just up and down. And mostly down.

. . .

[This is as far as I could recall/record of our rather elevated
conversation which took place a few days prior to my writing it
down. There are some notes at the end indicating he told some sort
of parable; and that my recounting of the parable resulted in Senya's
correcting my interpretation, "so you can properly record what I say
for others, since you like to write so much." And a little later in the

conversation, half way to the beach, perhaps to my joking reaction to his implications that I should be called upon to record & interpret him, he said with a mild laugh, "Marty, you don't know who I am." And then seriously, "It is not to be known my real identity, until I pass on from this world." (Not a preoccupation. I only heard him say this once.)]

Journal Notes

5/23/87 [Our 1987 trek across the states begins.]

Arriving in NYC Thursday, Senya style, "I'd prefer to call when we get there," cold. We went through nearly 2 dollars of quarters and a page of friends in nearly 2 hours, and ended up with a place to stay that night and possibilities for the next. That night, our friend for the night, John, who had known/met me for only an hour once before on St. Croix, warmed up to letting us stay indefinitely, and Friday morning 2 others panned out, one of them simply a stranger coming up on the elevator from walking his dog. So, in 24 hrs, we had 3 very nice places to stay between 2 of us, and still more possibilities to call if we wanted. New York, described as dangerous by both my father & my brother, seems so warm.

We took the bus to Queens subway, right on into our place. Carrying the box of books put a crook in my back. But all people along the way were so positive, helpful, and warm.

. . .

Jogging ~3 miles; to & around twice, Central Park's reservoir: I see/feel the huge warm flush of all these very old-familiar tree leaves. (I find this pen.) Only the white (or is it burr?) oak and linden leaves are not full sized. Only these, and the nippiness, and the blossoms of those trees yet blooming (one of them identical to the gnip we left blooming in St. Croix) indicate anything of yet still Spring. The rest says loudly, "Summer!" As I run around, passing all manner of runners & walkers, I find myself in compulsive habit saying to each one without a walkman in their ears, "Good morning," and beaming a great big, thrilled, seeming almost caricaturishly out-of-place smile at my excitement of being with the trees among whom I was raised; but all persons seem to take me as natural as nature, ... wanted or unwanted, ... slowly or fast.

On my way home down 83rd, I see what I didn't see on my way out: fat patches of tulips in the boulevard separation of—is it Lexington?—on both sides. All standing at crowded attention, denuded, every last pedal dropped, feminine parts showing, male lifeless residuals still hanging attached to few.

Summer belongs to the woman. Man can come along or not. She might miss one or a few here or there, but every woman owns summer. Us men think we are there and eat it up every year. But too many of us, I am afraid, don't know or take the care to find what she really is and raise the child only of our own imagination.

5/24/87 ... A conversation: Senya says havin all the other people affecting you, by writing letters & so—because that's what it all is, just people affecting each other—that makes you lose touch with who you really are, and you need to drop all that to find your true self (African essence). It also includes continually analyzing yourself with respect to your mother this and your father that. Drop all that. And let yourself be your self. I hear that.

Ironically it seems to mean also limiting contact with perhaps the most influential to me of all, right now—Senya himself.

A Pome 5/27/87

Travelling in NYC with Senya is a whole new city. "See the birds? Hear them? Which ones are they?" To my surprise I am able to name them. I must of travelled this way through here, myself, before. Only not so intently/totally!

And the trees! Same way. A hesitation, a hanging at a curb, foot out, perfect balance, no suggestion of motion except by shape, a dancer freeze. Following too close, I nearly step into his shoes.

A flute out at any moment, attracted by the acoustics, or the sounds already there. He hears every sparrow in the middle of traffic pulsing Park Avenue. And in the hum of the bus engine, ... "Hear the flute?"

"Look at that cloud. Look at these rocks. These are original. Ancient. Now this is my kind of park [St. Nicholas— gone bush]!"

The book this is binding in my skull to carry forever mine is huge hardbound, with a glossy jacket. Photos. Senya's The Nature Tour of New York ... on a double-decker shoes.

Journal Notes

6/2/87, Pennsylvania. We bussed, NYC to Bethlehem, & drove to Phila.. Again, too many places to stay. Set up with David for the night, late night, after open mic at Bacchanal. Then called Kim. Terry, her sister, was stayin up all nite if necessary for us to come by. It almost was & we stayed up & up discussin & musicin & lyin down to sleep on the floor, Senya & Atu talkin til dawn. But I fell asleep in the midst of instruments, human & otherwise, scattered on the floor, and woke up unknown hours later, the only human one around—in the <u>physical</u>. In the <u>spirit</u>, I was <u>all-one</u>, as we'd said and said all into the night.

———

There are two realms of existence that play about with each other inside our soul selfs. One is the individual, the inner self, including family and friends, however we might define that ourselves. The other is the world community at large, to which we belong, however comfortably or uncomfortably. Inside ourselves they banter. As Rashidah says, it is not either-or. It is all part of the same. One. Us. But a uniqueness of New York (City) I am fascinated with is that it is impossible to go out the door or look out the window, dirty or not, and not feel the immediate intimacy of the fact of HUGE WORLD COMMUNITY. So huge that you can run scared (back inside of a very small apartment, with no yard) and be crazy in the barriers you set up. Or you can fall easily into the fact and amazement of it all & take & be your part in as close to the <u>full</u> reality of it as perhaps anywhere else in the world. It is very imposingly inspiring, in the moment. But I'm not in this life sure about the long run.

6/4/87 (continuing from above) All the connections that could be made are so incredible that sometimes it seems like none of them are made.

———

    The path is not something you can do together.   (Perhaps.)

———

6/12/87, Washington, DC
    This is an attempt at a xerox copy of everything that you
        have written or said.
    It is an attempt. Just like yours. It is success.
    It is complete. It is already done before pen meets page.
    I seem to meet you. Not having ever separated.
    How can I even say thank you for joining me.

———

~6/13/87
    What do you do when you come out
    and meet a world already there?

A Song written by Senya and myself, 6/ 13 or 14 /87, at his parents' home in Washington, DC.

Town Bird

I. You might hear the sound
    Of wings flyin by
    And when you peer around
    Ain no ting in the sky
It's just that good ole fashion town bird
Flappin in yo ear.

II. When you move to the castle
    Better bring your frien along
    Cause every shook n hassle
    Gonna need that soothin song
That never set it down bird
That town bird in your ear.
(That always around bird
Town bird in your ear.)

III. When you walkin the city
    You might think you're flappin your wings
    But you ain flyin nowhere
    Without that town bird sings
That good ole good ole town bird
Town bird in your ear.
(That ever lost & found bird
Town bird in your ear.)

IV. Might be a pigeon
    Could be a hawk
    But don't care what region
    It is in which you walk
You better not go without
That town bird in your ear.

[Repeat Verse I.]

A Pome 6/20/87, Connecticut

Top

Sliding glass doors onto the porch,
Birds chirping above the traffic,
Unclear air,
Same bath towels as last time,
I awake at John's again.
I lean over and look down to see the twenty-three
        tiers of repeated balconies,
But see a dry needle & oak leaf throw rug over
        bedrock right up against my face.
Are these the same sparrows?

Standing back and stunned, I look out across at the
        old sea of tops of buildings,
But see only the tops and thighs of trees, both
        large and small, close and far, punk
        hairdo-ing the haystack mountain and friends
        across the valley. Laurel blooms in two
        shades.
Are these the same oaks, grown tall and towering?

Of the grid of streets and city blocks, all trace
        is lost. There is no pattern in the trees.
I squint & screen for the slightest sign of small
        toy cars below.
Are buildings lost in underbrush, as we had dreamed,
        in rooftop groves—in elevated, estimated,
        6 to 8 feet of top soil?

Spinning, I think out loud, "This could not happen
        within the week."
Am I the same man?

And John,
John;
How does he do this?

Journal Notes

6/23/87, Vermont. The first three entries are from pocket notes made during our full day's visit with Wawasiki Ashram leader, Nina.

You have to feel it*. Then you understand why you have to keep the master from feeling it*. You do that by repeating the Simran (learned at initiation).   {*the pain & sorrow of all the people living.}

———

You need a nother living nothing to take you out of you into it.

———

Marriage as the ultimate wish of every soul. [Marriage to the Master]

———

When you are ready, you have and see a dear friend go up and it does not cause you sadness. You then see it all before you. Next life will be your turn. Next life will be very comfortable and busy. You don't need to know this when it happens, or that it happened. [a random thought in responce to an incident in someone else's life, probably Nina's experience of the "loss" of her initial Master, Sant Kirpal Singh]

———

We are all capable of the most high [physical, material] capacity. Yet.
Only the ones who are not perfected are not sure. And they are right. That is not the way to go, nor the point.

———

I am struck by all the lavish, often self-built/self-designed homes we are visiting, burning wood for heat. All the people warmly taking us in, moving time aside in their lives, feeding us. John walking out along 10 years of 70 acres of home-known paths. And pristine Nina doing the same with 20 more years, and 7 more acres. Each a guru, each to a path of individuality, only the latter to the individuality of the lack of relationship in the total marriage of all, each individual, to the oneness of nothing which is love. And the other to the individuality of his coiled snake flag, "Don't tread on me."
     I am struck by how far & full you can go, with people warmly receiving you into their home, home to home, state to state, land to land.

———

6/30/87

What would I have been like if I had been brought up simpler. I think that is what I'm going to find out.

And that's what I will pass on to others younger. It is so easy to sit there and do nothing. Not have all those things thrown at us. And we are comfortable.

And is it possible we are wiser?

A Pome The Fifth of July morning, 1987, Vermont

Dawn's Early Light, Later On, Same Place

The whole cold darkness of silhouettes of huge tree-bodies,
The slate roof reflection of what little shine there is in what little sky,
The incessant prattle of at last allowed uninterrupted birds,
a monotone of species coming from seeming one tree,
a backdrop of ever present river roar, never heard before.
A robin pokes into the noise.
A black cat silent.
Semi truck whine on I-91.
Three garden plots as still as the minute hand of the kitchen clock,
hung over.
Smoke from the lumber kiln, only playing.
Even mosquitoes reluctant.
Brown Cat.
Nation.

Snowball bush, hollyhock watch unnoticed pear trees.
Nobody up.

Journal Notes

7/9/87, Ohio. On the road 50 days & for the first time I feel/meet the inner recall of self that so total sings and whistles so many songs and glee, on down the road, aimless & true.

———

Senya comin out of the Bells grocery store yesterday: "You're so totally excessive. We're very much alike. You're just like me." Today: "We went in to get a slight snack & came out with 4 shopping bags."

———

Miles and miles and miles and miles and miles and miles and miles and miles. What connections are you trying to make? Who do you want to meet? So often. So far. Where are you going, with all those miles?

Children, children, children, & children. What world are you having them for? What exactly are you passing on to your children? For what world? To go where?

A Pome 7/13/87, Indianapolis

Full Circle

Do you cry
as I cry,
but different
volumes, different
distances, different
viscosities down different
cheeks?

To seek self alone first,
to have to offer,
to be,
before giving
. . . another blunder?

To dive within,
the pool source (of tears)?

We have to leave:

An impossible known:
one must divide to unite.

Couldn't we do it smiling?

It's just the eyes
get in the way of the circle we'd
complete if we turned our
mouthcorners all the way up.

Journal Notes

8/4/87, Seattle. (with Ken) Look at the world as a non-competitive world & behave accordingly.

———

8/7/87 (with Winnie) Distractions—relationships.
You will go off by yourself when you have to.
Need to sheer off distractions and be honest and focus.

—— [8/21/87, Banff, Alberta, Canada. Senya left this plane.] ——

Two Pomes

8/22/87

> This come & go can get to be a bit much.
> But there is no man who came & go like Senya.
> In each of our lives he came & go so many times,
> Always the joy like he never had left,
> Or <u>more</u>, really—That's what he liked!
> Who will make the flutes, now?

8/28/87, Winnipeg, Manitoba, Canada

> There's always the why there's always the why
> there's always the why I'm here right now
> there's always the why there's always the why
> there's always the why I hear it in his smile
> there's always the why there's always the why
> there's always the why there's always the why
> I know where I'm going there's always the why
> there's always the why there's always the why
> there's always the why I'll see it in a while
> there's always the why there's always the why
> Years of working there's always the why
> there's always the why there's always the why
> there's always the why I feel like going
> there's always the why there's always the why
> But I think I'll stay there's always the why
> there's always the why there's always the why
> there's always the why

Journal Notes

9/22/87, Pennsylvania. There are those who know and seek out others by offerings, by signs, common as feathers. They watch your eyes when they hand it to you. And wait, sometimes for long times. One time you might connect, as they did, and went searching for others, and know.

Like Winnie, like Senya. Two people who were so tuned. And never met. And always are. In perfect speaking terms.

Here, here's a feather.

Stone or rock.

These things are given.

Shell.

Wood.

___

If I had left him as he was, I would have somewhere to return (and do). ...To make a flute of his "tigh" bone, was his instruction.* I feel now that if I had—if I had trusted him to the hilt, to the total—and how much was that? surely not too much to ask of anyone—if I had; the return visit would've had a new message for me, a new lesson along the road of my growth of spirit would've met me there, I am feeling now, if I only had, had left him there as he wished.* Something far more than a thigh bone, would wait.

I wonder if I have, by chosing to do otherwise, totally lost any chance of reaching this lesson-message. And further, I wonder if I have destroyed what message was layed by this man (who defies for me the word "man") for each other person he touched as he did touch.

Certainly not. Forgiveness & understanding were written in to his ever-present smile.

{*He expressed his wishes/instructions to a few close friends, several years prior.}

___

10/7/87, Home. St. Croix.
Senya went many places with white as well as Black. He was undenyably undenyingly Black, and universalist African. (Africa being, in fact, the seat of origin of all humanity.) He is a messenger to us all.

132

A Pome 10/6/87

while smiling

sound and light guide-gliding through the forest, without feet
without wings, wisening all it touches
a man hear-see-feeling each glance, a seeker
knowing his direction of truth
birds seem close onto the path, emitting
call-songs, high trills or low notes, some play
flutes in full flight, high above; some play
at rest on a branch, or the ground; some
while darting through the underbrush
this man knows them all, raises
bamboo flute to pursed mouth
and plays out all the cash in his heart
plays until it never stops, and never began, he
flies with the notes in the direction of all through & out
bending knees into the ground, flying; vibrating
each touched object's ear with
light
      his mischevious love-giving grin
      source of the bamboo tree he is playing
which is hearing, brilliant, beaming, light & sound as one.

V. Companions

August 21, 1987

this figure encompasses all

    today.

       on
we are all out

        a

       limb . . .

   which is ver
       y
        y
       y
          fragile.

  above all   we   love

            our life
            with it's

    pitfalls

       .

       .

        .

; it is an opportunity to RISE

      in love.

              — Naima Wade Rodriguez
              Quaking Grass Press
              Brattleboro, Vermont

IN MEMORY OF SENYA

The Island mourns Senya Darklight

who has gone to rest

No longer will his melodious sounds

encircle this Island of Paradise.

Boys and girls

swaying and chanting words

serene and beautiful

with Senya

whom they loved.

Goodbye, Senya Darklight

You and earthly things

have parted

for you have gone to a spirit beyond—

Rest!

— Cora Ramos, St. Croix

Senya

To a very very good fellow

who was always calm always mellow

helping those who were in need

very far from hate and greed

a man full of joy full of love

was Senya like a peacefull dove

full of hopes full of dreams

never thinking hurtful schemes

making friends both far and wide

never letting any of them slide

he was a very good man

so now he's resting in God's hand

— Sharae Joyce Curtis
St. Croix

SENYA

HE WAS WITH US
ONLY A LITTLE WHILE.
SEVERAL YEARS AS A UNITED STATES MARINE
    AND SAILOR
THEN THE PEACEFUL LIFE
CLOSE TO NATURE.
IN THE HILLS OF NORTH-WEST ST. CROIX,
HE PUT UP HIS TENT
AND LIVED QUIETLY UNDER THE MOON AND
    THE STARS.
IN THE STILLNESS OF THE NIGHT
HE PLAYED HIS FLUTE
AND THE SOUND FLOWED IN THE VALLEYS AND
    IN THE HILLS,
SWEET, FRESH, AND CLEAR
LIKE WATER RIPPLING THROUGH A GUT.
SO SWEET A SOUND,
BIRDS CHIRPED WITH DELIGHT,
WILD CATTLE ROARED WITH JOY,
AND EVEN DEER STOPPED AND LISTENED.
NOW THE QUIET, CARING SOUL
HAS FLOWN AWAY
TO ANOTHER SHORE.
OUR SENYA IS NO MORE!
HIS FLUTE IS SILENT;
HIS VOICE MUTE.
BUT HIS POETRY,
SOFT, DEEP, SWEET, AND GENTLE
AS RAIN DROPS,
WILL ALWAYS RING IN OUR MINDS
AND IN OUR HEARTS.

—Richard A. Schrader, Sr., St. Croix

This past weekend I learned my friend, Senya Darklight, died in a fall while mountain climbing in Banff Natl Park, BC. I'm missing him more now than when I heard. Senya didn't believe in death. I wrote and wrote about meeting Senya. Sharing with Senya. I was all memories of the realness of being with him. I feel honored our spirits laughed and danced together through a common shyness. Writing about Senya became an article, a photograph in words of living we labeled ... "come to a poetry reading." Senya wrote a poem, the title poem of his book, Rise in Love. Everywhere I went this weekend I recited the poem. Until I heard myself scream: "Senya you were to Rise Up the Mountain."

I read a piece titled "French Fries" about a bag lady who dreams of living at McDonalds. It's my favorite because it ends with light and dreams. "I'm part of that light, part of the whole sky ..." And Senya is saying yes yes with his body, his smile, his flashing red eyes surrounded by island dredlocks, ... "you got to have a dream. It's our dreams make us what we are." And Senya leads a rush of lovely applause. And Senya
is part of the light.

— Helen June Noble
Indianapolis, Indiana

RISE IN LOVE

Poet Senya, the flowers that grow
where you fell were bent over
for a few days only, where you
pressed them down that night you lay
most intently looking

upward at the shooting stars.
The wild red clover and the violet
mountain asters spring back,
as if you had been nearly
insubstantial,

you who came to every blossom
like the black bee that turns
suddenly silent when it gathers
its pollen. Though your book
remained on my shelf

for weeks after we met, I look
to it at last when I've been told
of how your body was found at
the base of a cliff in Banff,
Alberta after you went on alone
through the deepening

twilight. What was it, brother,
that you could see beyond
the summit, which took you
by surprise? I read your twelve
short poems under the title:
Rise in Love,

ironically at first, as I
picture you reading them on your
visit to Chicago, outloud
to still other unknown poets
in smoke-filled backrooms

overlooking the city, when what
you really wanted to say were
prayers for peace and silence.
But after the irony there follows
a glimpse of the shooting star
you might have seen.

I see it also, crossing the sky
with uncommon brightness and
duration, for there is always
more mystery than death in this
kind of flight. Senya,

I watch the sky tonight from
the lawn outside, and after seeing
the falling of a star, I go back
into my room and write this
elegy. Across inevitable

boundaries, I assure you that
you saw too much light to ever
be a successful poet in terms
of this world. And once you've
gone beyond the range

of sight, passing onward, inward,
and upward, you are a frail
yet beautiful messenger who has
simply delivered your message
and then returned

from whence you came. Unto
the Most High, I commend you,
beyond the stars we see with
our outer eyes: where the bee
is always a point

of light in darkness, falling
out of itself into still
undreamed of flowers in bloom.
There is a Sound beneath
the silence, and it will never
stop ringing.

— Michael Jewell
Worcester, Vermont

143

28 August, 1987
SENYA   by Somala Markaei
Grand Bay, Dominica

Rise, Senya is here.
Where? There, and every where.
National African
Born Trinidadian
Dread-locks Rasta name Senya
Senya's spirit shall make thy wonder.
Which are the moment thou shall fear?
The one who is near and always there?
Or the one so near, yet so far?
Oh death, where is your sting?
Oh grave, where is your victory?
Symbol point out Senya.
This moment I and I have come to share.
Tribute to the Poet Senya.
Which is the reason we all are there.
It have been written some where, in
I and I imagination.
There is no recognition for a living man.
Where is the love at I Father's command?
Senya went hunting on a snow mountain.
His memories has cause us to gather round.
Chanting and nahaibingaing "yea yah"
Senya come to St. Croix with nothing/
Gone with nothing.
Left something.
A moment we all come to share.
Tribute to the brother.
Love Rasta
Praise Selassie
Iry

144

Dear Marty,   8 Sept 87

Thinking of you with love. You are so constantly in our thoughts. I promised you I would write some thoughts at random.

One of my very beautifully spiritual friends said that she believed that when one climbs the ladder of spiritual growth, and reaches the top, they just step off in to a cloud. She had never met a person so near to the top of the ladder as Senya, she said.

I'm sure everyone that met him felt the same about him. When I told each one of my dear friends, that you met here, about Senya's leaving us, each person wept openly and with as much heartbreak as though he were next of kin to them. And so he was! To every one who knew him!

For myself I had never met a person who could look right into my soul and read me, as he could, with the exception of you and [son] Greg, and perhaps [grandson] Jamie. Strangely, each person who met him felt the same way.

Also, I felt instant and deep love for him, and deep happiness & joy with his sense of humour. He was so huggable to me. And again each person who met him felt the same way!

The power of his spirit is tremendous! It continues to pervade me with strength and peace, and I know it is so with you.

Senya had no hang-ups. He was totally happy with himself and _free_ to give pure love and help to his fellow man.

We all wept and continue to weep & mourn inwardly because we will have his presence no more in this physical world, _and_ (everyone mentioned this) because his passing is _such_ a _loss_ to this world that _needs_ him _so_ _dearly_! But perhaps his work was done.

Every one sends their love to you, Marty, and their concern for you for the trauma of it all. I know you feel Senya with you, strongly thru it all.

(The first 2 nights after your phone call, I couldn't sleep, and then I was aware of Senya's presence saying, "It's all right. Be at peace." and I went into the most relaxing sleep I've had in years. And strangely, my back, which has hurt me for years, hasn't hurt since.)

Bye for now, my _Precious_ Marty. Sieg sends his love with mine. Give Don and Barbara a hug for us.

                                    — ever loving you,
                                       Weezie

                          Louise Silver
                          Salmon Arm, B.C., Canada

Tues. 9/2/87
2:15 P.M.
for Senya Darklight
written 3 days after
Terry called to say he died.

So Senya has died—
moved onto another level
risen in love permanently.
Once again I am left behind
to weep and moan in private time.
Once again time ran out.
His body lay for three days
expired on breath
that fell 55 feet.
Now he flies back to his roots
for ancestral burial
Dust to dust, cloud to cloud
I hear his bamboo flutes
play his wind into songs
that stretch from St. Croix
to Nexus in Philadelphia
to Godfrey Daniels in Bethlehem
into the chambered caverns of
my heart pulsing with oxygenated
breath—
Keeping the rhythm
heartbeat to heartbeat
an unchained melody
eternal as any Dutchman
floating in limbo time.
Peace & Love, dear Senya,
Carol Ann

— Carol Ann Robertson
Philadelphia, Pennsylvania

146

WAKING FROM BILATERAL KNEE SURGERY

All my world a groggy haze filled with pain.
In my knees to be sure, so expected
But far worse and completely unexplained
Intense pain in my chest—made breast and breath
A reach for life that seemed to flee.
Intense pain in my right arm and shoulder
As though dislocated, misappropriated.
And my right eye watering for nearly forty-eight hours.
No reason. No explanation. No logic to all these
Morbid pains that made me wonder what happened during
The long hours of surgery. No sane way to understand
The turmoil and crushed feeling in my upper body until
The call, the letter and then the long talk with Marty.
Senya fell as I was waking from my surgery in recovery room.
Between the anesthesia and post-operative opiates
I felt Senya's fall and death, my body a mirror of his
Fatal injuries that spoke without words, that flew the
Distant miles, the distant mountains between us, that
Linked us in ways I nearly could not comprehend.
In the ether between Boston and Canada, Senya and I
Danced this most awesome and horrendous yet wondrous dance.
In this ether between Boston and Canada a mosaic of
Life and death mixed, then separated, filled me with the call
Lazarus returning from death, me returning from the unconscious.
In this time of roses and champagne, I remember, I remember
As I sip and feel the bubbles of life arise, I celebrate
     each journey—worlds within worlds
      without end
    a continual circle of dance and chance.

— Carol Ann Robertson
Philadelphia, Pennsylvania

147

THE POET

Everyone is a poet.
Even though they might not know it.
Poetry is no mystery.
The secret of the poem is it sincerity.
We all have something to say
in our own special way.
Whether we make it rythme or not,
write it or say it from the heart.
It is all the same.
Poetry is just another name
for expressing one's feelings and thoughts
without concern for the grammatical faults.
By using the beauty of words
the message of the poet is heard,
sometimes clear and understandable,
sometimes mysterious and full of parable.
But no matter what the poet states
or the poem particular taste,
the test of the poem is how to
express outwardly what is in your heart true.

— George Cannon, St. Croix

THE FLUTER AND THE MOUNTAIN

(In memory of my fellow-poet, Senya Darklight)

Out of the hills the Poet came with script and bamboo flute,
Like Robin out of Sherwood's glades, he headed for the feat.
His peers all gathered round to hear him chant his poetry
Which claimed the golden prize: a journey to a far country.
There he met the Mountain which challenged one and all,
To brave its cliffs to see if Nature would not them extol.
"If only I could peep into it's eyes," the Fluter thought,
"I'd gain that wonder light which hapless ponderers have sought."
So up and up he climbed to peer into the Mountain's eyes,
To grasp the secret of life's dark and dreary plights.
He hurried down to show the world that ken that he had found;
But fate stood in his way—soon he lay helpless on the ground.
He snatched his bamboo flute—some final feeble notes he blew;
But nobody was close enough to hear just what he knew.
His only friend, too far up on the cliff to hear him fall;
Unnoticed, passed him on the way as the Mount wrapped its shawl.
A Bard was lost—his secret perished with him in the dark,
In the bosom of the Mountain's side, where no fires spark.

—Mark Sylvester
Dominica and St. Croix

149

Senya

I couldn't, wouldn't think
about what I knew but didn't
want to know

Now, many months later, I
can't sleep, I get up and
think about knowing you

I can smell the oils so
familiar and sweet,
the look of your bright eyes
and playful mouth

I can hear the sound and
soft expressions in your deep voice
I can feel your touch and remember
how you knew about touch

I remember the way you
watched my baby grow
the way you loved her
the way she loved you
and climbed on you and
the way she touched your hair

I remember the music,
the way you freed me
to the music in my heart
the plans we made to play
in the old cistern, the bamboo
grove, the tapes we made
and had plans to make

I remember the laughter
A baby sliding down your guitar
something I would say,
you would say, something
else

I remember the times we would
talk for hours
the garden spot you cleared
for me and cut your hand

Senya, I miss you
I miss your smell
I miss your laughter,
Your voice, your music,
your wisdom
I hope you are happy

A rare bird lived near my
house for a couple of weeks
after your death
I never knew what kind it was
but its call was loud and clear

Senya, will I ever see you again?
Will we ever sit down over a cup
of lemongrass tea together again?
I have the cup Aunt Weezie
made for you.

I hadn't blown my flutes since
I heard … until tonight
It was as though I blew and
your spirit tumbled out all
around me, reminding me
and visiting me

If I play my flute again will
you visit me?
Is your spirit in the bamboo
you worked?

Ah Senya forgive me for thoughtless
words and for unsaid words like
I love you.

— Rita Gates
St. Croix

Dear Marty,

Amy just wrote me a letter telling me that Senya had died while mountain climbing.

I only met him once, for about an hour, through Earthwatch. In that single hour, however, Senya made more of a lasting impression than anyone else I have ever met.

He brought life to its natural level. Through what he said, his poetry, his music, and his lifestyle I saw many wonderful things. He had an amazingly clear perspective concerning the lifestyles that most people led.

Before leaving his tent, we played flutes for a little while. He offered me the flute I was playing. It is a walking stick which contains two flutes in one. I could tell that it meant a lot to him, but that it meant more that I accept it. I thanked him kindly for it and took the flute on the condition that I wouldn't let it sit and gather dust but rather play it to share with the rest of the world. So I play it (much to the annoyance of those around me) and I bring it where I go.

Just as we were leaving, I took a picture of Senya playing a flute. I know that I've given you copies of the image. One plane of him hangs on my wall. A photograph to remind me of the man, who he was and still is. People who see the picture ask who he is and I tell them what he is—a man who accomplishes much in life for he has found harmony with life.

I don't cry over Senya Darklight's death, for I understand that death is inevitable. But I feel strongly that the world will miss him greatly, whether the world realizes it or not.

Love,
Clayton Jones
North Falmouth, Massachusetts

This picture we took on the evening, just before we met together. It was near the tent-place, where we had the wonderful, with the spirit of love filled evening and morning with you!

The picture shows, "how near heaven and earth is together"—so Senya is not far away—and first of all, when we are together in thoughts. We'll never forget you and _Senya!_

Hedwig and Otto

Dear Marty,

... The remembrance of you and Senya—of our common time is so near for us and we felt the pain of loosing a good friend—a human, having thoughts, which are universally—(we can say this, in spite of knowing you only a short time—but it was a very precious and impressive time).
We also believe that Senya's spirit will be with us and maybe many people will read his poems and will start to live fuller and with more love for all our world!
... Marty, you are on the right way—but maybe, till finishing your "Companion to Senya" there will be some barriers or difficult situations. Please, Marty, take our praying to God, our thoughts to you and Senya's spirit, for encourage (cheer up?)—to go on this way. We think it is worth for Senya, for his deeply life and his examplary, open character (nature).
The only short time of meeting you made an deep impression on us. You, Marty, are the nearest companion to Senya—therefore your thoughts, your outlook on life is similar to Senya's. He has 'stamped' our and special (we think) your life.
Therefore your thoughts, your words ... are very valuable also (too)!
—> that means: worth for copyright.
The other way of life—a life in love, mutual "respect" ... peace ... a lot of people have forgotten. We must show them this way of life again.
You are able to do it in words ... and in practical life. We will try it—with our life—to bring your, Senya's— at least, God's light and spirit to the people. Marty, we will work together and we will be companions on this way. ...

Hedwig and Otto Larch, Wörgl, Tirol, Austria

SENYA

As Robert Frost said:
"I think I know what I've been doing
I've been going around
looking for kindred spirits
to comfort them and comfort myself
And that's all I'm doing anytime."

Senya seemed to comfort me more than me him
Yet sometimes when comforting a friend
we say truths we know but never said before
And then they serve both the comforted
and the comfortor

I also better heard thru him
(and now I hear him thru them)
the harmonius sounds of nature
The coo of a dove and its throatier cousin
the pigeon

The joyful chirps of banana quits, chincherees
pearl eyed thrushies and wailin blackbirds.
And I'll forever think of him
when I hear the screaming, piercing
freedom cries of the red tailed hawk.

And his eye(i)sight gave such insights
Hardly a flower ever went unnoticed
He could spend a whole day watching clouds
"Because they are so beautiful
somebody must pay them notice"

Along the beaches
He constantly collected shells

"Which have forever been there
waiting to be noticed"

He seemed to see and to be everything
just as everything saw and was (is) him.
His vision was "All in the Most High"
"I see hawk, hawk sees me
I am hawk, hawk is me"

Like all of us he had his tests
An infected tooth, a swollen eye
An angry neighbor who disturbed his sleep
envious of his tent and sleeping mat

To him these were samples of life's tests
To be looked upon
not as stumbling blocks
but as stepping stones

The tooth healed
the eye unswelled
And he yielded the mat
and massaged the feet
of the angry neighbor

He lived in the moment
When greeted by "What you been doin"
His response was:
"When I'm walkin, I'm walkin
when I'm talkin, I'm talkin
when I'm thinkin, I'm thinkin"

Bidding farewell, a friend said
"You take care" He replied
"I'll take care of the you in me
You take care of the me in you"

He wanted us to prepare
for our spiritual destination
Like one making airline reservations
carefully planning the journey ahead

So that when departure time arrives
Our reservations having been confirmed
We can pass peacefully on ...

Rather than suddenly be called
to depart without prayerfully planning
And thereby go to our destination
In chaos ...

I miss his physical presence
I have some flutes, poems, shells
photos, and a soundscape
as memorabilia

But his spiritual presence
lives in my many images of him
Within the flowers, birds, clouds
and hawks

In the sunlight
after a morning rain
When I see sparkling diamonds
on the leaves

When I image his mischievous smile
sometimes even in my dreams
As a welcome ally during a nightmare
... or anytime

— Cenzo, St. Croix

158

Excerpted from "Senya Reflects on Life as a Poet" *and* "Silent Flute, Poet Remembered", *from* The St. Croix Avis, *March 30 and August 30, respectively, 1987,* written by James Weeks Jr.:

Poetry, says Senya Darklight, comes in the rustle of the leaves, the whistling of the birds and the sound of the sea. It comes in silence—between gaps of conversation where there is no sound.

"When you walk along the beach and see the shells and the stones—footprints in the sand—all that is poetry," says the poet.

To him poetry "is life in its totality. It is beyond racism and classism. It exists in different stages and has no beginning or end."

... I ... headed deep into the hills of northern St. Croix. The scenery was beautiful. The moist smell of the rainforest wafted into my nostrils. Trees jutted into the heavens (or so it seemed).

But the roads were rough and my car was old. I prayed it wouldn't over-heat. I stopped by a roadside house after 20 minutes of driving. I tooted my horn and a dreadlocked sister came out.

... I was in luck. She knew where Senya lived and offered to take me there. I left my car by her house and we walked.

Together we eased through a barbed wire fence and made our way down a steep hill. The trees prevented the rays of the harsh afternoon sun from reaching our bodies. It was cool.

We crossed a stream on the bottom and proceeded up the opposite side of the hill. That's where my "guide" left me. I continued onward following the directions that she had given me.

I made a few more turns before finding his humble dwelling abode. It was a tent. A brown one—an old one, but still in good condition.

I heard no movements. "Senya," I bawled out.

He emerged shirtless. "Hail," he said as a smile overpowered his face. I returned the smile and we entered his home.

We sat on the floor. A thin covering blanketed the floor. The ground was hard. I longed for a chair but there was none.

Clothes were neatly hung in one corner. Home made cooking utensils rested near a coal pot. A sleeping bag rested by his feet.

Nature provided some music and Senya provided the rest of it with his flute. A mountain dove cooed sensually.

Senya giggled and recited "Music Is." "Music is a message that can set us free/ Music can take us all from where we are to where we all should be/ Listen to the music/ Let it liberate your mind/ Journey with the music beyond space and time/ Life and sound wrapped in one..."

He stops in the midst of it and begins a short monologue about poets and poetry past and present. In the past, he says, people were better listeners; they were more attentive, and hence—had sharper memories.

I nodded my head in agreement. He smiled. ...

[After moving from Trinidad to Washington DC,] the condition of his family greatly disturbed him .... He saw how poverty crushed people ... communities ... nations. It forced him to make decisions about how he would live his life and what his values would be.

"I didn't feel much to be a part of the role that everybody else played in the world. My mind was to live a quiet life—to seek knowledge of myself so that I could understand why all this madness was going on," he recalls.

"I got to really see how people could get stuck in a little groove that feels comfortable to them and spend the rest of their lives doing it. They stop growing," he adds.

He pauses momentarily and continues: "A person shouldn't have to kill themselves making a living. They should have time to put towards inner growth.

"It's good to be alive on the earth," he tells me in that gentle voice of his. "Every moment is precious; every instant is special. Our lives could be forfeited at any time. It (death) could be just around the corner.

"Why do trifling things?" he asks as he twirls a strand of dreadlocks between his fingers. "Why get caught up in superficial, meaningless interaction? Why not really appreciate life and do the things that make sense.

"It makes some sense to put some energies toward spiritual things—towards developing our humaneness, our livingness and compassion—dropping all the lower vices and getting attached to the virtues of living a balanced, harmonious life."

The hills of northern St. Croix grants him the peace of mind necessary to write poetry and reflect on life. Last year he published a book of poems entitled "Arise In Love." He would like to publish more if the finances are available.

He seeks simplicity. "I don't see life in a possessive term. I'm not looking to get my piece of the rock or a piece of the earth. I know that my needs will be met as long as I keep doing works that are acceptable to God. I know that I'll have sustenance for my body and a place to rest my head."

"The major work that everyone faces is with themselves. It's not a matter of trying to reform others or reform society. Self mastery is the key. Most people are content to be masters of others instead of themselves. If we can reform ourselves then we can inspire others to do likewise," he explains philosophically.

He walks to the corner and retrieves something from a bag. It's a wooden flute. "This is for you."

160